APR 7 1997

The Securities and Exchange Commission

The Securities and Exchange Commission

Philip Koslow

CHELSEA HOUSE PUBLISHERS

On the cover: The floor of the New York Stock Exchange.
Frontispiece: An SEC staff attorney at work in the agency's New York regional office.

Chelsea House Publishers
Editor-in-Chief: Nancy Toff
Executive Editor: Remmel T. Nunn
Managing Editor: Karyn Gullen Browne
Copy Chief: Juliann Barbato
Picture Editor: Adrian G. Allen
Art Director: Maria Epes
Manufacturing Manager: Gerald Levine

Know Your Government
Senior Editor: Kathy Kuhtz

Staff for THE SECURITIES AND EXCHANGE COMMISSION
Associate Editor: Scott Prentzas
Copy Editor: Brian Sookram
Deputy Copy Chief: Nicole Bowen
Editorial Assistant: Elizabeth Nix
Picture Research: Dixon & Turner Research Associates, Inc.
Picture Coordinator: Melanie Sanford
Assistant Art Director: Loraine Machlin
Senior Designer: Noreen M. Lamb
Production Manager: Joseph Romano
Production Coordinator: Marie Claire Cebrián

First Printing

1   3   5   7   9   8   6   4   2

Library of Congress Cataloging-in-Publication Data

Koslow, Philip.
    The Securities and Exchange Commission/Philip Koslow.
        p.   cm.—(Know your government)
    Bibliography; p.
    Includes index.
    Summary: Surveys the history of the SEC with descriptions of structure, current function, and influence on United States society.
    ISBN 1-55546-119-0
            0-7910-0905-X (pbk.)
    1. United States. Securities and Exchange Commission—Juvenile literature.
[1. United States. Securities and Exchange Commission.]   I. Title.   II. Series: Know your government (New York, N.Y.)   89-15757
HG4910.K655   1990   CIP
353.0082′58—dc20   AC

CONTENTS

KNOW YOUR GOVERNMENT

CHELSEA HOUSE PUBLISHERS

INTRODUCTION

Government: Crises of Confidence

Arthur M. Schlesinger, jr.

From the start, Americans have regarded their government with a mixture of reliance and mistrust. The men who founded the republic did not doubt the indispensability of government. "If men were angels," observed the 51st Federalist Paper, "no government would be necessary." But men are not angels. Because human beings are subject to wicked as well as to noble impulses, government was deemed essential to assure freedom and order.

At the same time, the American revolutionaries knew that government could also become a source of injury and oppression. The men who gathered in Philadelphia in 1787 to write the Constitution therefore had two purposes in mind. They wanted to establish a strong central authority and to limit that central authority's capacity to abuse its power.

To prevent the abuse of power, the Founding Fathers wrote two basic principles into the new Constitution. The principle of federalism divided power between the state governments and the central authority. The principle of the separation of powers subdivided the central authority itself into three branches—the executive, the legislative, and the judiciary—so that "each may be a check on the other." The *Know Your Government* series focuses on the major executive departments and agencies in these branches of the federal government.

The Constitution did not plan the executive branch in any detail. After vesting the executive power in the president, it assumed the existence of "executive departments" without specifying what these departments should be. Congress began defining their functions in 1789 by creating the Departments of State, Treasury, and War. The secretaries in charge of these departments made up President Washington's first cabinet. Congress also provided for a legal officer, and President Washington soon invited the attorney general, as he was called, to attend cabinet meetings. As need required, Congress created more executive departments.

Setting up the cabinet was only the first step in organizing the American state. With almost no guidance from the Constitution, President Washington, seconded by Alexander Hamilton, his brilliant secretary of the treasury, equipped the infant republic with a working administrative structure. The Federalists believed in both executive energy and executive accountability and set high standards for public appointments. The Jeffersonian opposition had less faith in strong government and preferred local government to the central authority. But when Jefferson himself became president in 1801, although he set out to change the direction of policy, he found no reason to alter the framework the Federalists had erected.

By 1801 there were about 3,000 federal civilian employees in a nation of a little more than 5 million people. Growth in territory and population steadily enlarged national responsibilities. Thirty years later, when Jackson was president, there were more than 11,000 government workers in a nation of 13 million. The federal establishment was increasing at a faster rate than the population.

Jackson's presidency brought significant changes in the federal service. He believed that the executive branch contained too many officials who saw their jobs as "species of property" and as "a means of promoting individual interest." Against the idea of a permanent service based on life tenure, Jackson argued for the periodic redistribution of federal offices, contending that this was the democratic way and that official duties could be made "so plain and simple that men of intelligence may readily qualify themselves for their performance." He called this policy rotation-in-office. His opponents called it the spoils system.

In fact, partisan legend exaggerated the extent of Jackson's removals. More than 80 percent of federal officeholders retained their jobs. Jackson discharged no larger a proportion of government workers than Jefferson had done a generation earlier. But the rise in these years of mass political parties gave federal patronage new importance as a means of building the party and of rewarding activists. Jackson's successors were less restrained in the distribu-

8

tion of spoils. As the federal establishment grew—to nearly 40,000 by 1861—the politicization of the public service excited increasing concern.

After the Civil War the spoils system became a major political issue. High-minded men condemned it as the root of all political evil. The spoilsmen, said the British commentator James Bryce, "have distorted and depraved the mechanism of politics." Patronage, by giving jobs to unqualified, incompetent, and dishonest persons, lowered the standards of public service and nourished corrupt political machines. Office-seekers pursued presidents and cabinet secretaries without mercy. "Patronage," said Ulysses S. Grant after his presidency, "is the bane of the presidential office." "Every time I appoint someone to office," said another political leader, "I make a hundred enemies and one ingrate." George William Curtis, the president of the National Civil Service Reform League, summed up the indictment. He said,

> The theory which perverts public trusts into party spoils, making public employment dependent upon personal favor and not on proved merit, necessarily ruins the self-respect of public employees, destroys the function of party in a republic, prostitutes elections into a desperate strife for personal profit, and degrades the national character by lowering the moral tone and standard of the country.

The object of civil service reform was to promote efficiency and honesty in the public service and to bring about the ethical regeneration of public life. Over bitter opposition from politicians, the reformers in 1883 passed the Pendleton Act, establishing a bipartisan Civil Service Commission, competitive examinations, and appointment on merit. The Pendleton Act also gave the president authority to extend by executive order the number of "classified" jobs—that is, jobs subject to the merit system. The act applied initially only to about 14,000 of the more than 100,000 federal positions. But by the end of the 19th century 40 percent of federal jobs had moved into the classified category.

Civil service reform was in part a response to the growing complexity of American life. As society grew more organized and problems more technical, official duties were no longer so plain and simple that any person of intelligence could perform them. In public service, as in other areas, the all-round man was yielding ground to the expert, the amateur to the professional. The excesses of the spoils system thus provoked the counter-ideal of scientific public administration, separate from politics and, as far as possible, insulated against it.

The cult of the expert, however, had its own excesses. The idea that administration could be divorced from policy was an illusion. And in the realm of policy, the expert, however much segregated from partisan politics, can never attain perfect objectivity. He remains the prisoner of his own set of values. It is these values rather than technical expertise that determine fundamental judgments of public policy. To turn over such judgments to experts, moreover, would be to abandon democracy itself; for in a democracy final decisions must be made by the people and their elected representatives. "The business of the expert," the British political scientist Harold Laski rightly said, "is to be on tap and not on top."

Politics, however, were deeply ingrained in American folkways. This meant intermittent tension between the presidential government, elected every four years by the people, and the permanent government, which saw presidents come and go while it went on forever. Sometimes the permanent government knew better than its political masters; sometimes it opposed or sabotaged valuable new initiatives. In the end a strong president with effective cabinet secretaries could make the permanent government responsive to presidential purpose, but it was often an exasperating struggle.

The struggle within the executive branch was less important, however, than the growing impatience with bureaucracy in society as a whole. The 20th century saw a considerable expansion of the federal establishment. The Great Depression and the New Deal led the national government to take on a variety of new responsibilities. The New Deal extended the federal regulatory apparatus. By 1940, in a nation of 130 million people, the number of federal workers for the first time passed the 1 million mark. The Second World War brought federal civilian employment to 3.8 million in 1945. With peace, the federal establishment declined to around 2 million by 1950. Then growth resumed, reaching 2.8 million by the 1980s.

The New Deal years saw rising criticism of "big government" and "bureaucracy." Businessmen resented federal regulation. Conservatives worried about the impact of paternalistic government on individual self-reliance, on community responsibility, and on economic and personal freedom. The nation in effect renewed the old debate between Hamilton and Jefferson in the early republic, although with an ironic exchange of positions. For the Hamiltonian constituency, the "rich and well-born," once the advocate of affirmative government, now condemned government intervention, while the Jeffersonian constituency, the plain people, once the advocate of a weak central government and of states' rights, now favored government intervention.

In the 1980s, with the presidency of Ronald Reagan, the debate has burst out with unusual intensity. According to conservatives, government intervention abridges liberty, stifles enterprise, and is inefficient, wasteful, and

10

arbitrary. It disturbs the harmony of the self-adjusting market and creates worse troubles than it solves. Get government off our backs, according to the popular cliché, and our problems will solve themselves. When government is necessary, let it be at the local level, close to the people. Above all, stop the inexorable growth of the federal government.

In fact, for all the talk about the "swollen" and "bloated" bureaucracy, the federal establishment has not been growing as inexorably as many Americans seem to believe. In 1949, it consisted of 2.1 million people. Thirty years later, while the country had grown by 70 million, the federal force had grown only by 750,000. Federal workers were a smaller percentage of the population in 1985 than they were in 1955—or in 1940. The federal establishment, in short, has not kept pace with population growth. Moreover, national defense and the postal service account for 60 percent of federal employment.

Why then the widespread idea about the remorseless growth of government? It is partly because in the 1960s the national government assumed new and intrusive functions: affirmative action in civil rights, environmental protection, safety and health in the workplace, community organization, legal aid to the poor. Although this enlargement of the federal regulatory role was accompanied by marked growth in the size of government on all levels, the expansion has taken place primarily in state and local government. Whereas the federal force increased by only 27 percent in the 30 years after 1950, the state and local government force increased by an astonishing 212 percent.

Despite the statistics, the conviction flourishes in some minds that the national government is a steadily growing behemoth swallowing up the liberties of the people. The foes of Washington prefer local government, feeling it is closer to the people and therefore allegedly more responsive to popular needs. Obviously there is a great deal to be said for settling local questions locally. But local government is characteristically the government of the locally powerful. Historically, the way the locally powerless have won their human and constitutional rights has often been through appeal to the national government. The national government has vindicated racial justice against local bigotry, defended the Bill of Rights against local vigilantism, and protected natural resources against local greed. It has civilized industry and secured the rights of labor organizations. Had the states' rights creed prevailed, there would perhaps still be slavery in the United States.

The national authority, far from diminishing the individual, has given most Americans more personal dignity and liberty than ever before. The individual freedoms destroyed by the increase in national authority have been in the main

11

the freedom to deny black Americans their rights as citizens; the freedom to put small children to work in mills and immigrants in sweatshops; the freedom to pay starvation wages, require barbarous working hours, and permit squalid working conditions; the freedom to deceive in the sale of goods and securities; the freedom to pollute the environment—all freedoms that, one supposes, a civilized nation can readily do without.

"Statements are made," said President John F. Kennedy in 1963, "labelling the Federal Government an outsider, an intruder, an adversary. . . . The United States Government is not a stranger or not an enemy. It is the people of fifty states joining in a national effort. . . . Only a great national effort by a great people working together can explore the mysteries of space, harvest the products at the bottom of the ocean, and mobilize the human, natural, and material resources of our lands."

So an old debate continues. However, Americans are of two minds. When pollsters ask large, spacious questions—Do you think government has become too involved in your lives? Do you think government should stop regulating business?—a sizable majority opposes big government. But when asked specific questions about the practical work of government—Do you favor social security? unemployment compensation? Medicare? health and safety standards in factories? environmental protection? government guarantee of jobs for everyone seeking employment? price and wage controls when inflation threatens?—a sizable majority approves of intervention.

In general, Americans do not want less government. What they want is more efficient government. They want government to do a better job. For a time in the 1970s, with Vietnam and Watergate, Americans lost confidence in the national government. In 1964, more than three-quarters of those polled had thought the national government could be trusted to do right most of the time. By 1980 only one-quarter was prepared to offer such trust. But by 1984 trust in the federal government to manage national affairs had climbed back to 45 percent.

Bureaucracy is a term of abuse. But it is impossible to run any large organization, whether public or private, without a bureaucracy's division of labor and hierarchy of authority. And we live in a world of large organizations. Without bureaucracy modern society would collapse. The problem is not to abolish bureaucracy, but to make it flexible, efficient, and capable of innovation.

Two hundred years after the drafting of the Constitution, Americans still regard government with a mixture of reliance and mistrust—a good combination. Mistrust is the best way to keep government reliable. Informed criticism

12

is the means of correcting governmental inefficiency, incompetence, and arbitrariness; that is, of best enabling government to play its essential role. For without government, we cannot attain the goals of the Founding Fathers. Without an understanding of government, we cannot have the informed criticism that makes government do the job right. It is the duty of every American citizen to know our government—which is what this series is all about.

New York City's Wall Street as it appeared in 1894. Wall Street, the site of the New York Stock Exchange (NYSE), is the financial center of the United States. The Securities and Exchange Commission was created in 1934 to regulate securities exchanges such as the NYSE.

ONE

Other People's Money

The Securities and Exchange Commission (SEC) was created by Congress in 1934 to regulate the securities markets and to protect the interests of investors. *Securities*, the general name for stocks and bonds, play an important role in the economy of the United States. When new businesses are started or existing corporations need money to expand, they often raise money by inviting the public to invest in their operations. In order to do this, the companies issue stocks and bonds, which they sell to investment banks—banks that specialize in the underwriting of newly issued securities. These banks then sell the securities to the public through licensed brokers.

Securities of the largest U.S. corporations are bought and sold by brokers on the New York Stock Exchange (NYSE). The NYSE, located on Wall Street in New York City, lists the stocks of more than 1,600 companies. As of 1989, 606 brokerage firms were members of the exchange. It handles about 80 percent of the securities trading in the United States. Smaller companies are represented on the American Stock Exchange (AMEX), also located in New York City, and on the over-the-counter (OTC) market, a nationwide computerized system operated by the National Association of Securities Dealers (NASD). All three exchanges, as well as smaller regional exchanges, function under the supervision of the SEC.

Approximately 40 to 50 million people own securities in U.S. corporations. The total value of those securities is estimated to be $2 trillion. Owners of a

Stock certificates are issued to investors when they buy shares of a company's stock. A share of stock represents part ownership in the company. The SEC monitors the information that is made public by companies offering stocks to investors to ensure that it is accurate.

company's securities are legally part owners of the company, and they are entitled to a cash dividend when the company makes a profit. Generally speaking, the owner of one share of stock has one vote at shareholders' meetings. However, because large corporations may have tens or even hundreds of millions of shares of stock in circulation, the average investor has little influence on corporate decisions. Most people buy stock because they believe they will be able to sell it for more than they paid. Sometimes they are right, and sometimes they are wrong. "Playing the market," as people like to call it, always entails an element of risk. The behavior of the securities markets can be influenced by a host of political and economic factors—and sometimes by nothing more than the day-to-day mood of investors. Even professional analysts can be mistaken in their predictions, and when they are, private investors and large firms alike may lose many millions of dollars.

The one thing all investors have a right to expect is that the entire system is honest and fair. That is, they have a right to expect that the risks they are taking are absolutely the same for everyone else who is trading in the markets. They have a right to expect accurate information about the companies in which they are investing. They have a right to expect that brokers, to whom they are paying a fee on every transaction, will execute their orders faithfully. They have a right to expect, finally, that no individual will be able to manipulate the system for his or her benefit at the expense of the vast majority. Congress established the SEC to make sure that these expectations are realized whenever securities are traded in the United States.

With as many as 200 million shares of stock changing hands during a busy day on the NYSE alone, the work of the SEC is detailed and complex. The staff of the SEC spends the bulk of its time enforcing the securities laws, analyzing data from the securities markets, regulating mutual funds and investment advisers, and counseling investors who have complaints about their brokers. The SEC is also responsible for overseeing the stocks, bonds, and financings issued by public utilities, such as gas and electric companies, and for protecting the rights of investors when companies go into bankruptcy. These activities are usually reported in the business section of the newspaper, not on the front page. In the late 1980s, however, the enforcement and market-regulation functions of the SEC propelled the agency into newspaper headlines.

- In 1986 agents of the Justice Department, acting on the basis of evidence gathered by the SEC, swept into Wall Street offices and arrested stock traders for engaging in *insider trading*. Insider trading occurs when someone buys or sells stock on the basis of important information not available to the public, and for this reason it is a violation of the securities laws. In the cases brought to light by the SEC investigators, the traders were able to learn from inside sources (who were paid for their information) when certain firms were about to become the objects of takeover bids by other companies. The stock prices of both companies increased as soon as the bids were made public; by buying early at lower prices and then selling when the price rose, the insiders were able to make healthy profits. Because buying stock in the hope of a takeover is not in itself illegal, it is often difficult to prove that a transaction was based on inside information. The SEC was widely praised for the pains-taking detective work that led to prison terms for investment banker Dennis Levine and stock trader Ivan Boesky, as well as a $650 million penalty against the prominent investment firm of Drexel Burnham Lambert Inc.

- Stock prices crashed on Black Monday—October 19, 1987—threatening the funds of millions of investors and the economic well-being of the United

17

Investment banker Dennis Levine leaves court in 1987 after being convicted of securities fraud, perjury, and tax evasion. Levine was sentenced to two years in prison and fined $362,000; the SEC was applauded for its investigation of Levine's activities.

States. The SEC worked closely with the NYSE and the Federal Reserve Board, which regulates the flow of money in the banking system, to prevent a total collapse of the markets. The SEC then conducted an extensive analysis of the crash and published its findings in an 847-page report. On the basis of this report, the agency asked Congress to extend its powers of market regulation.

Those who followed these news stories might have taken for granted that the securities markets have always operated under public supervision. However, from the founding of the NYSE in 1792 to the passage of the Securities Act in 1933, no such supervision was exercised in the United States. Government and business leaders believed that the exchanges had a vested interest in maintaining the confidence of investors and thus would see to it that

Original members of the NYSE trade among themselves in 1792, under a buttonwood tree facing 68 Wall Street. Today, brokers who trade securities must be registered with the SEC.

the activities of their members were honest. Investment bankers were assumed to be the best judges of the soundness of stock-issuing companies. These assumptions were not unreasonable, and there are those in the business community who still endorse them. But assumptions can be fallible in the real world, where human frailties play a large role—and this faith in the markets did not prevent a harrowing progression of business "panics" from occurring at frequent intervals: 1837, 1853, 1857, 1869, 1873, 1893, 1907.

The causes underlying these panics were complex. However, large-scale manipulations of the stock market definitely played a major role in all of them. It was not uncommon, for example, for an unscrupulous group of stock traders to form a "pool." They would buy a large amount of a particular stock and then cause it to appear highly valuable by trading back and forth among themselves. Eventually other investors would begin to clamor for shares of this apparent money-maker; the price of the stock would go sky-high, and the pool members could sell for a great deal more than the stocks had cost them. Without the pool members to pump up the market, however, prices would soon fall, and the more recent buyers would suffer a loss.

Alternatively, conspirators could drive prices down by carefully staged bouts of short selling—known as *bear raids* in reference to *bear market,* a market in which stock prices are consistently falling. When practiced by individuals, short selling is a legitimate way of trying to make money in a declining market by selling stock one does not own. The short seller "borrows" stock from a broker—paying a fee for the service and agreeing to return the stock by a specified date—and then sells the stock at the going rate. If the price of the stock goes down, the short seller can buy back the amount of shares due the broker, return them, and come away with a profit. Of course, if the market should rally and the price goes up, the short seller loses money. As with any other investing technique, short selling is based upon expectations, not certainties. But whenever a group of powerful investors staged a bear raid by selling short in concert, they could guarantee that the market would behave the way they wanted it to. That is, they were able to drive prices down by the sheer volume of their sales and by the fear they inspired in other investors. When the market got low enough, the "bears" could then buy the stock at bargain rates to cover their short sales. They reaped enormous profits while others were wiped out.

When unlucky or unwary investors were caught in the jaws of pools and bear raids, the banks that had lent them money went under as well. And without the capital provided by banks, businesses failed. People then lost their jobs and had no money to feed their families. Fortunately, prosperity always returned. The

United States was rich in land and natural resources and had a large supply of cheap labor that was constantly renewed by immigrants from Europe. But the question had to be asked: Was there not a more sensible way of managing the nation's financial affairs?

European governments had generally decided that there was a solution, and they passed laws as early as the 1840s regulating the trading of securities. But in the United States the spirit of individualism dominated political thought throughout the 19th century. There was no organized working class to pressure the government for reforms, and the idea of public regulation of business was slow to catch on. Industrial expansion and the development of the country were the paramount goals. Despite the chaos of business panics, people still looked upon the stock market as a kind of national poker game; the shrewdest players went home with their pockets bulging, and too bad for the rest. The cynical bravado of the 19th-century "plungers," as they were called, was perfectly expressed by speculator Jim Fisk, who shrugged off criticism

Jim Fisk (1834–72) made a fortune in stock manipulations that ruined the Erie Railroad. He also cooperated with financier Jay Gould in an attempt to corner the gold market in 1869, causing a nationwide depression.

21

after one of his many financial schemes caused the market to crash in 1869: "A fellow can't have a little innocent fun without everybody raising a halloo and going wild." Despite the outcry in the press on this and other occasions, the government rarely stopped anyone from having "fun" at the public's expense.

Government regulation of economic affairs finally gained acceptance in the United States at the beginning of the 20th century. Presidents Theodore Roosevelt and William Howard Taft enforced new laws against trusts, combinations of companies that fixed prices and stifled competition. Crusading reporters known as muckrakers exposed such evils as the exploitation of workers, the wasting of natural resources, and the sale of impure foods and drugs, and Congress passed laws to curb these practices. President Woodrow

A cartoon from the early 1900s shows President Theodore Roosevelt on Wall Street, battling the giants Jay Gould, James J. Hill, J. P. Morgan, John D. Rockefeller, Sr., and the Oxnard Brothers, who were among the nation's most influential financiers and industrialists.

President Woodrow Wilson won passage of an impressive array of progressive measures that provided significant federal regulation over commerce. In 1913 he signed the Federal Reserve Act, which reorganized the American banking and currency systems.

Wilson's reform-minded administration (1913–21) oversaw the creation of the Federal Reserve System, the Federal Trade Commission (FTC), the Food and Drug Administration (FDA), and the Department of Labor. But still the stock market remained untouched, except for the blue-sky laws—which required financial disclosures by companies issuing securities—enacted by various states. (The laws got their nickname when a Kansas legislator noted that unwary investors often ended up owning a piece of the blue sky and nothing more.) In New York, which often has set the pace in social legislation, a committee of the state legislature investigated the banking and securities industries for six years. The committee exposed abuses and recommended disclosure laws but inexplicably concluded that the markets were best left to their own devices.

This hands-off approach continued in the years after World War I, when the stock market ceased to be the private preserve of the rich. Ordinary people all over the country, 4 or 5 million in all, began to invest their money in stocks. They found that they could buy on margin, or credit, putting down as little as 10 percent in cash and borrowing the rest from a stockbroker. The stockbroker borrowed money from the bank in order to finance his customers' purchases. The more buyers there were, the higher the prices of stock went, and profits piled up as if by magic. Americans believed throughout the 1920s that the old boom-and-bust cycles were relics of the past. They saw the Jazz Age, with its easy money, sleek motorcars, rakish fashions, and lavish parties, as the wave of the future.

It took almost a decade for the reckoning to come. In 1929 the most devastating stock market crash in the history of the United States took place. Surveying the wreckage, people began to understand that without any guidance or restraints the system was bound to go out of control. As had happened with every wild surge in the past, the market eventually reached a point where the prices of stocks far exceeded the financial strength of the companies behind them. Then the most astute traders began to sell large amounts of stock, intending to take their profits while the market was still high. Prices then began to level off, prompting other investors to get edgy and sell in turn. Before long, what was once a buying craze turned into a selling craze as everyone tried to get out before it was too late.

But in order to sell something you have to own it. Those who were buying on margin had always paid their debts out of the profits they made as stock prices steadily increased. Suddenly, they were asked to put up hard cash to cover their loans or else watch the value of their stocks plummet until they were altogether worthless. Similarly, brokers were pressed to pay their bank loans, and the banks that had lent more than they had in their vaults found themselves insolvent when borrowers defaulted and panicked depositors flocked in to demand their money. Without the money provided by banks and investors, businesses failed by the thousands. By 1933, at the lowest point of the Great Depression, almost 25 percent of the work force was unemployed.

When President Franklin D. Roosevelt took office in 1933, the country was prepared for decisive action. Roosevelt responded with the New Deal, a wide-ranging program of economic and social reform. In requesting securities laws from Congress, Roosevelt declared: "What we seek is a return to a clear understanding that those who manage banks, corporations, and other agencies handling or using other people's money are trustees acting for others."

Sporting the latest Jazz Age fashions, a young couple enjoys a jaunt in Washington, D.C. Americans experienced a new level of prosperity during the 1920s, but the boom ended in 1929 when the stock market crashed.

Congress agreed. The Securities Act of 1933 set strict standards for companies issuing stock. In the following year, Congress created the SEC.

During the SEC's first years, three extraordinary individuals served as chairman of the agency. Joseph P. Kennedy, one of the few millionaires to support the New Deal, sold the idea of federal regulation to the business community. James M. Landis, a Harvard-educated lawyer who helped draft the securities laws, developed an approach to regulation that made the SEC a model of efficiency and effectiveness. William O. Douglas, who later became a Supreme Court justice, engineered a decisive confrontation with the NYSE and established the SEC as a powerful force on Wall Street.

During World War II, the work of the SEC took a backseat to the war effort, and in the prosperous 1950s the agency found it difficult to break new ground. But the election of John F. Kennedy to the presidency in 1960 brought a renewal of interest in the SEC. Kennedy, the son of the agency's first chairman, increased the SEC's budget, and Congress broadened the agency's powers. After Kennedy's assassination in 1963, support for the SEC fluctuated throughout the 1960s and 1970s. Still a tiny agency compared with other

On the day following Black Monday in October 1987, these investors watched with concern as stock quotations were displayed outside a brokerage firm in New York City.

government bodies, the SEC often struggled to cope with securities markets that were growing and changing with unprecedented speed.

During the 1980s, the very principle of government regulation was called into question by the administration of President Ronald Reagan. The SEC eased some of its restrictions while vowing at the same time to crack down on illegal activity. The securities markets responded to deregulation and the general probusiness atmosphere in Washington with an explosion of activity that reminded people of the 1920s. The comparison proved all too accurate on Black Monday, when stock prices plunged wildly and the country appeared to be on the brink of another disaster.

However, the stock market did not collapse in 1987, and the economy did not sink into another depression. Nevertheless, small investors and large Wall Street firms alike suffered losses estimated at $500 billion of stock value. People expressed a renewed interest in preventing such violent and destructive fluctuations. And they were deeply troubled about the failure of personal ethics that in some cases led outwardly respectable people such as Dennis Levine and Ivan Boesky into criminal activities.

In this atmosphere of rapid change and moral uncertainty, the SEC is challenged to provide firm leadership for the 1990s and beyond. In order to maintain its reputation as the government's most successful regulatory agency, the SEC will have to strive for the energy and innovation that characterized its earliest years.

President Franklin D. Roosevelt's New Deal—a program designed to solve the economic problems created by the Great Depression—produced legislation that sought to eliminate questionable financial practices by regulating banks and the stock market.

TWO

The Cop on Wall Street

Franklin D. Roosevelt was inaugurated as president on March 4, 1933, and instituted a vigorous program of economic recovery and reform. During the first 14 weeks of Roosevelt's administration—a period that became known as the First Hundred Days—Congress passed an unprecedented amount of major legislation. These laws enabled the government to set up new agencies and implement programs for industrial recovery, public-works projects, relief benefits for the poor, rural electrification, social security, unemployment insurance, and dam construction in areas devastated by the droughts of the 1920s. Roosevelt's New Deal marked the acceptance by the American people of the idea that the government must take responsibility for the general well-being of the nation.

Roosevelt made securities legislation a major item in his legislative program. Despite a number of studies and congressional hearings that exposed serious abuses such as pools and bear raids in the securities markets, the previous administration, led by President Herbert Hoover, had never found the will to grapple with Wall Street. In 1933, four years after the crash, the markets remained in a dismal slump. Roosevelt knew that unless he could restore confidence in securities, which provided companies with the capital necessary for expansion, he had little chance of revitalizing American industry. Accord-

President Roosevelt's young Brain Trusters Benjamin Cohen (left) and Thomas Corcoran (right). Cohen and Corcoran, along with James Landis, became known on Capitol Hill as the Happy Hotdogs, a pun on the name of their mentor, Harvard Law School professor Felix Frankfurter.

ingly, he began to plan for new securities legislation only hours after winning the election.

Roosevelt's group of advisers, known as the Brain Trust, attempted to draft the securities act, but their efforts did not satisfy the president. Roosevelt finally gave the assignment to three men recommended by his former teacher, Professor Felix Frankfurter of the Harvard Law School: Benjamin Cohen, Thomas Corcoran, and James M. Landis. All three men were in their thirties. Cohen and Corcoran had both practiced law on Wall Street; Landis, then the youngest professor in the history of the Harvard Law School, was the first in the country to teach a course on business regulation. Together, the three men commanded a deep theoretical and practical knowledge of the securities industry.

The new, young members of the Brain Trust made their headquarters at 3238 R Street, NW, in Washington. This address became fixed in the public imagination as the Little Red House in Georgetown, a mysterious den where laws to change America were hatched. Actually, the house was quite large, having once been used by President Ulysses S. Grant as a summer White House. Now it was filled with young people who had flocked to Washington in order to participate in the New Deal. Frank Watson, a lawyer who worked for a number of different agencies, later recalled living in the Little Red House: "None of us made big money, but it was a time when everybody was broke and we made, for young fellows our age, very good money. . . . We didn't have expensive tastes, but we did run a household on the most inefficient system you could think of. . . . The house was old and poorly insulated. The coal came in there by the ton, and it didn't seem to last a week a truckload."

The first securities bill drafted by Cohen, Corcoran, and Landis was guided through the House of Representatives by Sam Rayburn of Texas. Rayburn, who was to serve almost 50 years in the House and who became one of the most powerful figures in Washington, was then chairman of the Committee on Interstate and Foreign Commerce. This committee was pivotal to the passage of most of the New Deal legislation. Roosevelt's program was essentially based on Article I, Section 8 of the Constitution, which empowers Congress to regulate commerce with foreign nations, between the states, and with Indian tribes. Without the approval of Rayburn's committee, there was little chance that Congress would pass the new laws. Rayburn, a staunch supporter of the

---

Sam Rayburn was responsible for the passage of much of the New Deal legislation and helped guide Roosevelt's securities bill through the House of Representatives. Rayburn later served as Speaker of the House for 17 years, the longest tenure in history.

New Deal, worked closely with Cohen, Corcoran, and Landis throughout the First Hundred Days. He made sure that the administration's bills were drawn up in the right way, and he ironed out objections within the committee. Under Rayburn's guidance, the committee approved the securities bill with a unanimous vote.

When the bill got to the floor of the House, the leadership announced that only five hours of debate would be allowed. There was only mild protest over this restriction, because nearly all the members agreed that legislation was necessary. The bill called for full disclosure by companies issuing new stock. Disclosure was to be made in a registration statement describing the issuing company's business operations and financial condition as well as the nature of the securities and their relation to other securities issued by the same company. The law mandated an interval of 20 days between the filing of the statement and the sale of the securities. During this time the SEC could demand clarification of any deficiencies in the statement and had the power to delay or even suspend the sale.

The proposed law was intended to supplant the various state blue-sky laws, which were recognized to be largely useless because they could not regulate stocks sold across state lines. The members of the House also understood that the bill had been drawn up with great care and skill, though Rayburn later joked, "I don't know if it passed because it was so damned good or so damned incomprehensible." The House passed the bill by a simple voice vote, and the Senate followed with quick approval. On May 23, 1933, President Roosevelt signed the Securities Act into law.

Creating an Agency

Even as the Securities Act of 1933 was taking effect, its proponents realized that it had two major flaws: It did not cover stocks already on the market and did not regulate the operation of the exchanges. Furthermore, the new law was being enforced by the Securities Division of the FTC. The FTC had been created in 1913 to investigate and prohibit unfair methods of competition such as agreements between large firms to fix prices and to squeeze out smaller competitors. But the FTC had never developed into an effective agency. It had difficulty defining its objectives, and its investigative and decision-making procedures prevented it from acting swiftly. Many members of Congress were openly contemptuous of the FTC and did not want to entrust it with the important job of implementing the new Securities Act.

Senator Francis Maloney of Connecticut, a vocal supporter of New Deal securities legislation.

As it happened, James Landis was running the Securities Division of the FTC and doing a good job. Ordinarily, this might have been enough to win over Congress. But curiously enough, the business community also began lobbying for a new agency. Although they had never feared the FTC, many business-people feared Landis, who had a reputation as an antibusiness radical. They felt that if they could get a new agency created, it might turn out to be less restrictive and diligent than Landis's office.

Despite the various pressures for change, some members of Congress disliked the idea of setting up a new authority over business. During the debate over the proposed Securities Exchange Act, Representative Fred Britten of Illinois openly declared his distrust of Cohen, Corcoran, and Landis, "the youthful legislative wizards from the little red house in Georgetown." He accused them of having the same ideas as the leaders of the Communist government in the Soviet Union, which had abolished all private business. The whole point of the legislation, Britten asserted, was "to Russianize everything worth while." But in the end it was Senator Francis Maloney of Connecticut who summed up the prevailing mood of the Congress: "I have no faith in a business confidence that is so tender a plant that it cannot stand the sunshine of immediate curative legislation for admitted existing abuses. . . . The truly dangerous radical in times like these, when all the plans of a generation are standing at the forks of the road, is the disbeliever in our power to control our own economic destiny."

Although there was a more extended debate this time, both houses of Congress passed the Securities Exchange Act in June 1934 by wide margins. With this law, Congress formally established the SEC and delineated its powers. According to the major provisions of the law:

- All securities exchanges in the United States would be required to register with the SEC and provide all information requested by the agency.
- All margin requirements (how much of the purchase price of a stock an investor may borrow from a broker) would be set by the Federal Reserve Board as part of its overall regulation of the money supply and interest rates (during the 1980s, margins were generally set at 50 percent).
- The use of securities as collateral for bank loans would be restricted.
- The concerted buying and selling tactics used in pools and bear raids would be prohibited.
- The ability of brokers to trade on their personal accounts would be subject to rulings by the SEC.
- All securities listed on the various exchanges would be registered with the SEC, and the companies issuing them would have to publish annual reports prepared by independent accountants.
- All exchanges and all brokers would be expected to keep detailed records, subject to inspection by the SEC.
- The SEC would have the right to suspend trading in a security at any time and also to suspend the operations of an exchange.
- The SEC could bring civil suits against offenders and could refer cases to the Justice Department for criminal prosecution.

President Roosevelt signed the bill into law on June 6, 1934, and the SEC was officially born. In the words of humorist Will Rogers, the government had finally "put a cop on Wall Street."

First Steps

Everyone in Washington assumed that Roosevelt would turn the tables on the business community and appoint James Landis as chairman of the new SEC. With his recent experience as head of the Securities Division of the FTC, Landis certainly knew more about securities regulation than anyone in the

The commissioners of the SEC met for the first time on July 2, 1934: (left to right, seated) Ferdinand Pecora, Joseph P. Kennedy (chairman), and James M. Landis; (standing) George Mathews and Robert E. Healy.

country. But the president had a knack for confounding his supporters as well as his opponents. He did pick Landis to be one of the five commissioners of the new agency, along with George Mathews of the FTC, congressional counsel Ferdinand Pecora, and Thomas Healy, a Vermont judge with a background in securities law. As the fifth commissioner—and chairman—Roosevelt chose Joseph P. Kennedy.

This was an absolute bombshell. Both the press and Roosevelt's own supporters were incredulous. In their eyes, Joe Kennedy was exactly the kind of operator the SEC was supposed to put out of business. He had made a fortune on Wall Street during he 1920s and lived like a king in the midst of the depression. Kennedy had been wise enough to sell his stocks well before the crash and had then devoted himself to politics. Unlike most businessmen, however, he was an ardent Democrat. The son of a Boston saloonkeeper, Kennedy had experienced the scorn and prejudice directed toward the Irish around the turn of the century, and he never lost his sympathy for the underdog. He believed that Roosevelt and his New Deal were the best hope for all those suffering from the depression. Kennedy had made large contributions to Roosevelt's campaign fund and traveled on Roosevelt's special train during the election campaign. Now, in 1934, it appeared that Roosevelt was choosing a highly inappropriate way of paying off a political debt.

In fact, the president had a very different motive. His first priorities were to pull the country out of the depression, to get the factories running, and to put people back to work. Roosevelt knew that he could never accomplish his objectives without the cooperation of business leaders. He had to convince them that the New Deal was good for business and good for the country before they would support his programs. And who could convince them better than one of their own? Kennedy knew what went on in the mind of businesspeople; he could talk to them in their own language. Landis, with his academic background, never could do this. Landis fully understood Roosevelt's thinking and approved of the appointment of Kennedy. He, at least, did not share the whimsical picture of the SEC's commissioners painted by the *Magazine of Wall Street*: "Four men in deadly earnest, chiefed by a good fellow, wise-cracker, successful speculator, high-liver—homes in Bronxville, Cape Cod, and Miami—generous spender."

Kennedy's style was certainly unusual for the head of a major government agency. Milton Katz, Kennedy's executive assistant, remembered the advice Kennedy gave him on how to negotiate with the leaders of the NYSE: "When you deal with those fellows you know what you've gotta do? You've got to force their mouths open and go in with a pair of pincers and just take all the gold out of their teeth." And when William O. Douglas was summoned to Washington to fill an important post at the SEC, he got a surprise when he asked the chairman for instructions. As Douglas recalled in his autobiography, *Go East, Young Man*, Kennedy replied, "Instructions? If I knew what to do, why in hell would I get you down here?"

Ultimately, people understood that Kennedy's offhand manner with subordinates was a sign of his confidence as an administrator. He recruited talented people, and he was not afraid to give them a free hand in doing their work.

The SEC began with a staff of 696 and a budget of $2.3 million. Because of the depression and the large number of talented young people coming to Washington, it was not difficult to fill the offices in the SEC building at 1758 Pennsylvania Avenue, NW, only a block and a half from the White House. "They poured in from all over the country," Douglas wrote, "coming by freight and bus and Pullman cars, some hitchhiking, some walking. They were filled with idealism and fervor. The best of our men and women were available by the thousands. They literally begged to work for us at the SEC."

The work load at the new agency was so enormous that in the first year the staff put in many hours of unpaid overtime. Douglas recalled that the regular working day lasted from 9:00 A.M. to 6:00 P.M.; many staffers took a two-hour break for dinner and then resumed work until midnight. During 1934 alone the SEC registered 24 stock exchanges, 2,400 securities firms, and 51,000 separate securities traded on the major exchanges. In the course of the year the agency closed down 10 small exchanges, including the New York Mining Exchange and the Boston Curb Exchange, both known for promoting securities of often dubious value. Under authority granted by the Securities Exchange Act, the SEC in its first year also investigated 2,300 cases of suspected fraud.

At the same time, Chairman Kennedy never lost sight of the SEC's other goal, the encouragement of honest business. Through public speeches and meetings with the leaders of the securities industry, he repeatedly made the point that the purpose of the SEC was not to control the industry. On the contrary, the point of its operations was to restore the public's confidence in the markets and to stimulate the flow of capital needed to fuel economic recovery.

Wall Street responded to Kennedy's assurances. In 1934, U.S. companies issued $643 million in new securities; the following year, the total rose to $2.7 billion. The SEC was so successful under Kennedy that even his previous opponents were sorry when he announced in 1935 that he was stepping down. *Time* magazine observed Kennedy's retirement by declaring that the SEC had "won [the] distinction of being the most ably administered New Deal agency in Washington."

The Landis Years

Now that the SEC had gotten off the ground, James M. Landis was the logical choice to replace Kennedy. A completely different personality, Landis was a brilliant scholar and lawyer who lacked a flair for press relations and political maneuvering. Douglas, who respected Landis but did not seem to have been fond of him, remembered him as an "intense, humorless man." Landis was a tireless worker and drove himself so hard that he rarely went home before midnight and sometimes even slept on a cot in his office. Landis was the principal architect of the SEC. He had suggested the key elements of the new securities laws, and as commissioner and chairman he set the standards for the agency's staff, worked out its basic procedures, and enlisted the support of private accountants in reporting financial data. Landis's foresight was largely

37

James M. Landis

From Franklin D. Roosevelt's New Deal to John F. Kennedy's New Frontier, James M. Landis helped shape the direction and growth of the Securities and Exchange Commission and other federal regulatory agencies. Landis, renowned for his keen intelligence, persuasiveness, and compulsive work habits, became the most influential figure in the history of the regulatory process.

Landis began working for the government in 1933 when President Roosevelt called him to Washington to help modify the proposed securities legislation. The original bill had met with strong opposition in Congress because it contained many loopholes and vague provisions. Landis, a Harvard Law School professor who specialized in the legislative process, assumed the task of redrafting the liabilities and enforcement provisions of the bill. He improved the original legislation by devising the stop order, a procedural device that prevented corporations from issuing stocks until they fulfilled all registration requirements. He also drafted the section that made corporate executives personally liable for violations of the act.

Congress passed the revised bill in May 1933. The Federal Trade Commission (FTC)—the agency originally responsible for enforcing the Securities Act—then asked Landis to prepare the complicated regulations for corporations to follow when registering their stock issues. In October, Landis was named a commissioner of the FTC, where he worked diligently to prevent Wall Street interests from weakening the securities laws. Meanwhile, Congress, dissatisfied with the Securities Act and with the FTC's inadequate enforcement of it, passed the Securities Exchange Act of 1934. The new act—which Landis helped draft —strengthened the securities laws, provided for the regulation of securities exchanges, and established the Securities and Exchange Commission. Roosevelt appointed Landis one of the commissioners, and Landis conceived and developed many of the legal procedures and administrative practices that the SEC followed in regulating the securities industry.

In 1935, at the age of 35, James Landis became chairman of the SEC. Under Landis, the SEC continued its policy of fostering cooperation between business and government. The aim of the SEC, beyond policing the exchanges to prevent fraudulent activity, was to strike a successful balance between maintaining the confidence of the business community and achieving Roosevelt's goal of restoring a sound economy. Landis also worked hard to establish effective regulation over the powerful holding companies that controlled the securities of many public utility companies. However, he was attacked from both the Right and the Left. Conservatives thought that Landis was a threat to business, and liberals charged that he should take

38

stronger action to protect investors, such as forbidding brokers from trading on their own accounts. Growing weary of the personal criticisms and the internal struggles over regulatory policies, Landis resigned as chairman in 1937 to become dean of Harvard Law School.

Landis continued to work for the government as a consultant. Most of his assignments—with agencies such as the Treasury Department and the War Department—involved solving intricate economic or organizational problems. In 1946, President Harry Truman appointed Landis chairman of the Civil Aeronautics Board (CAB), the agency responsible for regulating air commerce and transportation.

In 1960, President-elect John F. Kennedy commissioned Landis to prepare a study of the regulatory agencies. In what became known as the Landis Report, Landis attributed the gradual decline of the agencies to the poor quality of appointees during the Truman and Eisenhower administrations (1945–61). He believed that "good men can make poor laws workable," and "poor men will wreak havoc with good laws." He advocated increasing the power of commission chairmen.

Landis joined the Kennedy administration in February 1961 as special presidential assistant to help implement his recommendations. He devised specific plans to reorganize virtually every regulatory agency and called for greater presidential oversight of regulatory policies and decisions. His plans encountered fierce opposition in Congress, which voted down the proposals for most agencies, including the SEC. Landis had proposed that the SEC be reorganized to give the chairman more substantial policy-making power. The chairman could then delegate less important work to the SEC staff. Congress did accept the proposals for the FTC, the CAB, and the Federal Power Commission, and some of Landis's ideas were adopted in subsequent legislation. Landis resigned in June 1961 to return to his private law practice, but his illustrious career ended in disgrace when he pleaded guilty to income tax evasion in 1963.

James M. Landis at work at the SEC, where he spent many hours developing agency procedures. Landis, the principal architect of the SEC, became chairman in 1935.

responsible for the exceptional ability the SEC has demonstrated in doing a big job with a relatively small staff, year after year.

For all the fury with which he worked, Landis was really not the wild-eyed radical so dreaded by the business community. He had realized very early that the SEC could not possibly run the securities industry. In the first place, this would have required a vast and cumbersome bureaucracy. Landis, Cohen, and Corcoran had all shared the view, summarized by historian Michael Parrish, that "large organizations, public and private, could deaden individual responsibility and retard innovation." Landis had also learned by studying the failures of the FTC that it was ineffective to wait for businesses to do something wrong and then intervene to stop or punish them. Abuses must be prevented from ever occurring. Following Landis's ideas, the securities laws gave the SEC power to prevent a security from being sold until the SEC was satisfied that everything about it was in order. This arrangement compelled everyone involved in the marketing of a security to understand the laws and obey them, and it allowed the SEC to police the securities industry with only a fraction of the personnel that direct control would have required.

The effort to reform the NYSE, which all the SEC commissioners felt was essential, proved to be a far more difficult task. The so-called Old Guard, a group of traders who had been rich enough or shrewd enough to survive the 1929 crash, still controlled the exchange. They detested Roosevelt, the New Deal, and most of all, the SEC. There was so much hostility to regulation on Wall Street that when the SEC commissioners visited the NYSE in 1934, exchange president Richard Whitney brought in security guards to protect them.

Whitney behaved on that occasion as a proper host but was himself the leader of the resistance. Whitney was a figure of tremendous authority both on Wall Street and in the public imagination. He was tall and athletic, with aristocratic looks and manners. Like President Roosevelt, Whitney came from a socially prominent family and had been educated at the exclusive Groton School in Connecticut and at Harvard University. His older brother, George, was a leading partner in J. P. Morgan & Company, the most powerful financial institution in the United States. With the backing of the Morgan bank, Richard Whitney had unsuccessfully tried to rally the market on Black Thursday, October 29, 1929, by charging onto the trading floor and calling out orders for large blocks of stock.This dramatic gesture, widely reported in the press, made Whitney a folk hero, and during the depression he became the symbol of Wall Street's determination to restore its fortunes and lead the country back to prosperity. He was a formidable opponent, and throughout Landis's tenure Whitney battled every attempt by the SEC to change the administration of the NYSE and to eliminate unfair practices in stock trading.

Franklin Roosevelt won the 1936 election, defeating Alfred Landon in a landslide. The privileged social class into which Roosevelt had been born may have considered him a traitor, but the American people in general showed that they approved of him and his reforms. Nevertheless, when the stock market began to decline again in 1937, many people blamed the SEC for being too strict in its regulatory approach. The NYSE was quick to seize on this shift in public opinion, and its leaders defied the SEC more than ever. Despite Landis's deep commitment to the SEC, he appeared to have little taste for the imminent fight with the NYSE leadership. When Harvard Law School asked Landis to become its new dean in 1937, he accepted the post, and William O. Douglas succeeded him as chairman of the SEC.

The NYSE in 1934. When the SEC commissioners first visited the NYSE that year to investigate alleged abuses, the exchange president provided security guards to protect the commissioners from hostile traders.

Douglas's Victory

William O. Douglas was much closer in temperament to Kennedy than to Landis. He was as much a legal scholar as Landis, having taught at Yale Law School and written extensively on the legal aspects of finance. But he had been raised in the state of Washington and had worked on harvest crews during his summer vacations; the rough-and-tumble characters he had known in the work camps had provided him with a unique view of social problems and a taste for blunt speech and direct action. While serving as an SEC commissioner, Douglas had never tried to hide his impatience with Landis's cautious approach to regulation and distaste for confrontation. When Douglas became SEC chairman, he was determined to push through a program of stock exchange reform.

SEC chairman William O. Douglas accused floor traders of aggravating the ups and downs of Wall Street. In November 1937, he told members of the NYSE to prepare for substantial government intervention unless the traders themselves stablized the stock market.

43

Douglas made his intentions clear in a lengthy, carefully prepared press release issued on November 23, 1937. "Operating as private membership associations, exchanges have always administered their affairs in much the same manner as private clubs. For a business so vested with the public interest, this traditional method has become archaic." Douglas described the specific abuses to which the SEC objected, and he presented statistics to document the harm to the market that these abuses caused. The principal problem, as the SEC saw it, was that *floor traders* were in control of the NYSE. Floor traders were those who purchased seats on the exchange—for six-figure sums—and then bought and sold stocks strictly for themselves. The stock manipulators of the past, who had done so much damage to the market and the economy, had always been floor traders. *Commission brokers*, on the other hand, were those who traded stocks for their customers and earned their living by charging a commission, or percentage of the total price, on each transaction. The SEC wanted commission brokers to control the NYSE, even though commission brokers were not without faults. Some of them were known to

A stockbroker of the early 1900s examines stock quotations on the ticker tape in his office.

"churn" their customers' accounts, that is, to make unnecessary trades simply to increase their commission income. But the commission brokers, in the eyes of the SEC, had more of an interest than floor traders in the needs of investors and the general health of the market.

Douglas made it clear to the commission brokers that churning would not be tolerated. He also proposed a rule forbidding commission brokers from trading on their personal accounts, thus operating in effect as floor traders. (This is one rule that the SEC has never been able to enforce, despite the logic behind it—but the SEC does have absolute authority over all other activities of brokers.) Douglas argued, with the support of his statistics, that the sudden decline of the stock market in 1937 (the issuance of new securities had dropped by 50 percent from the previous year because of a general slowing down of the economy) was the result not of SEC regulation but rather of the manipulation of stock prices by floor traders, who were up to their old trick of organizing bear raids. He suggested that the NYSE would be wise to act quickly on its own, unless it wanted the SEC to step in and run the exchange.

Douglas was able to take a strong line because he had allies within the NYSE. A group of commission brokers, calling themselves the Elders, had been trying for some time to unseat the Old Guard on the NYSE's governing committee. But Richard Whitney had always beaten back their challenges. Even with Douglas backing the Elders, Whitney might have held firm for many more years if not for a scandal that, in Douglas's words, "delivered the stock market into my hands."

To the shock of the business community and the country at large, Whitney was forced in 1938 to declare his investment firm bankrupt. If it had only been a matter of making unwise investments, the event might not have been so damaging. But when the firm's books were examined, Whitney emerged as little more than a common embezzler. He had used his clients' money and securities to finance his own business schemes, and he had even dipped into the money set aside by the NYSE for the benefit of deceased members' families. Whitney pleaded guilty to charges of grand larceny and was sentenced to 5 to 10 years in prison. As John Brooks put it in his popular history of Wall Street in the 1930s, *Once in Golconda* (Golconda was a legendary city in India where everyone got rich): "Wall Street could hardly have been more embarrassed if J. P. Morgan had been caught helping himself from the collection plate at the Cathedral of St. John the Divine."

Douglas was not content with the arrest and conviction of Whitney. He insisted on holding hearings in Washington to explore the entire situation at the NYSE. For two and a half months, SEC attorneys grilled members of the

45

Richard Whitney (right), president of the NYSE (1930–35), arrives in court in 1938 to plead guilty to a charge of grand larceny. Whitney led Wall Street's opposition to government regulation of the securities markets.

exchange, trying to uncover evidence of a wider complicity in Whitney's schemes. They found what they were looking for. Both George Whitney, Richard's brother, and Thomas W. Lamont, the managing partner of the Morgan bank, admitted that they had strongly suspected some illegal activity on the part of Richard Whitney but had done nothing about it. In their way of looking at the world, Richard Whitney was a member of their private club, and the other club members felt that their duty to him was more important than their duty as financial officers and citizens.

If the public had ever doubted Douglas's claim that the NYSE was a corrupt institution, here was the proof. The Old Guard finally gave way, and the Elders pushed through the reforms they had agreed upon with Douglas. Henceforth, the NYSE would have a paid president who would not be allowed to trade in securities. Three members of the public would have seats on the governing committee, and commission brokers would make up a majority of the committee. The new committee set strict rules for the conduct of all stock exchange members, and these rules are still in effect today. The program worked so well that although there have been many securities frauds perpetrated in the United States since 1938, the NYSE itself has never again been touched by any scandal.

The industrial expansion created by the entry of the United States into World War II—such as aircraft production at the Vought-Sikorsky plant in Connecticut—stimulated economic recovery but diminished the perceived need for the SEC.

THREE

Decline and Rebirth

When President Roosevelt appointed William O. Douglas to fill a vacancy on the Supreme Court in 1939, the Securities and Exchange Commission was at its zenith. The agency's staff had increased from 696 to 1,678, and its budget had more than doubled. In 1939 the SEC had jurisdiction over 20 stock exchanges and 7,000 investment firms. By all appearances, it had established itself as a progressive force in the federal government and in American life.

In 1935, Congress had passed the Public Utility Holding Company Act, which gave the SEC authority to revamp the entire system under which public utilities, such as gas and electric companies, were owned and financed. In 1938 the Maloney Act, named after Senator Francis Maloney of Connecticut, extended the SEC's regulatory power to the OTC market, the nationwide network of brokers who handle transactions of stocks and bonds that are not listed on an exchange. And in 1940, Congress further increased the power and responsibilities of the SEC by passing the Investment Company Act and the Investment Advisers Act. The Investment Company Act authorized the SEC to register companies engaged in stock trading and gave the agency broad powers to supervise the selection of officers in these companies, their methods of doing business, and their relations to investors. The Investment Advisers Act likewise refined the Securities Exchange Act of 1934 by spelling out the

During his presidency (1945–53), Harry S. Truman concentrated on foreign affairs and on his unsuccessful attempt to gain enactment of his social reform program, the Fair Deal. Consequently, the SEC received little attention.

SEC's authority to register individual brokers, set standards for their performance, and monitor their compliance with the law. Although the later laws did not enjoy the same smooth passage as the 1933 and 1934 acts, Congress clearly supported the SEC.

When the United States entered World War II in 1941, however, the position of the SEC changed dramatically. The mobilization of the country's resources for the war effort immediately took precedence over everything else. Securities regulation was placed on the back burner, and the SEC was even obliged to pack up and move to Philadelphia in order to free up office space for the war-related agencies that were being created.

While the war was in progress, the SEC was largely limited to the technical function of monitoring the stock markets, which were not especially active. The SEC's staff was cut by 500, and any new initiatives by the agency were out of the question. American industry was working around the clock to turn out tanks, ships, and aircraft for the armed forces—media advertisements played up these themes—and neither Congress nor the public was worried about the regulation of business practices. When President Roosevelt died in April 1945, the SEC also lost its greatest champion.

The new president, Harry S. Truman, stated publicly that he did not understand the workings of the stock market and doubted that it was all that important. By implication, he did not think the SEC was all that important, either. He was in no hurry to bring the SEC back from its "exile" in Philadelphia after the war ended in 1945, and the agency did not return to Washington until 1948. And then it did not move back into its old quarters near the White House. Instead, the agency was assigned to a temporary building on Second Street and Indiana Avenue, NW, a neighborhood described by the *New York Times* as "one of the shabbiest sections of Washington." The building itself, which had been put up during the war, was so unimposing that SEC staffers began to call it "the tarpaper shack." The SEC occupied these quarters for 18 years.

The staff would probably not have minded the tarpaper shack so much if they had received any encouragement from the White House. They had undoubtedly hoped that President Truman, as he gained experience in office, would change his opinion about the importance of the securities markets. Apparently he did no such thing. The SEC commissioners that Truman appointed—he made nine appointments in all between 1945 and 1952—tended to be people who were in line for political favors rather than experts in securities law or business regulation. Indeed, Harry McDonald, a banker from Iowa whose main

Harry McDonald, chairman of the SEC from 1949 to 1952. Many of President Truman's appointees to the SEC reflected his disinterest in regulation of the securities industry. Congress was also unwilling to pass new regulatory legislation or to increase the SEC's budget so it could operate effectively.

experience had been financing dairy farms, candidly admitted his lack of qualifications when Truman appointed him SEC chairman in 1949: "My election as chairman . . . was a complete surprise to many, including myself."

During the years 1953 to 1961, when Dwight D. Eisenhower was president, the SEC reached its lowest ebb. It was not merely that Eisenhower was a Republican and the SEC was the brainchild of the Democrats. The Republicans admitted that the SEC was the model of what a government agency ought to be. Even the securities industry, for its part, had come to realize that the SEC was more of a help than a hindrance. Investors felt that if the SEC allowed a stock to be sold it must be all right—even though the agency had always been careful not to pass judgment on the value of a stock, only on the proper disclosure of details about the issuing company. Thus, the SEC's supervision provided free of charge a measure of public confidence that would have been difficult for a company to secure with any amount of advertising or public relations.

The Republicans, however, were not comfortable with the idea of government regulation. Even in the depths of the depression, they had always insisted that the economy would recover on its own. They might not go so far as to try to dismantle the SEC, but on the other hand they were not going to help the agency extend its powers. In addition, Eisenhower had committed himself to reducing the federal budget. Consequently, the SEC found its funds reduced year after year until, by 1955, it had only 696 employees—30 fewer than the number with which it had started 20 years earlier.

The 1950s was a period of prosperity for a majority of Americans as the United States emerged as the dominant industrial power in the world. It was a time when large corporations—such as General Motors, U.S. Steel, General Electric, and IBM—were expanding their operations and issuing more stock to raise capital. Despite the growing volume of stock being traded, the SEC was reduced by budget cuts almost to the role of a spectator. In 1955, for example, the SEC was able to inspect the records of only 1,000 of the 4,100 registered brokers; it obtained only 7 convictions for fraud and the suspension of only a single stock issue. And with its reduced staff, the SEC was virtually helpless to crack down on abuses such as the sale of stock in western uranium mines that turned out to have little uranium in them.

The SEC's reputation was further damaged when agency officials left to take jobs in the securities industry. This is a sore point in the world of the regulatory agencies. It inevitably raises the question: How diligent will an official be in regulating an industry if there is the prospect of a higher-paying job in that industry? The Ethics in Government Act of 1978 currently limits the ability of

Scientists using the IBM 1620 Data Processing System, which was designed in 1959 for scientific and engineering computations. During the 1950s, companies such as IBM issued large amounts of stock to finance the expansion of their businesses.

former officials to represent businesses on government-related issues. No such laws existed in the 1950s, because no one had ever imagined that the type of person who worked for the SEC or other reform-minded agencies would ever choose to enter the business world. The ease with which allegiances were shifted in the 1950s showed how profoundly the atmosphere in Washington had changed since the days of the New Deal.

Rebirth in the 1960s

When John F. Kennedy won the presidential election in 1960, he made it clear that the SEC would be resurrected. For one thing, President Kennedy was the son of the agency's first chairman, and it can be assumed that he got quite a bit of encouragement from his father. Furthermore, as a Democrat, he shared his party's belief in vigorous action by the federal government. He established a firm link with the New Deal tradition when he asked James Landis, who had helped with his election campaign, to write a report on the regulatory agencies and recommend improvements. Landis found most of the agencies in a run-down state, with low morale and outmoded procedures. He recommended sweeping reorganization and increased powers for agency heads. Landis's report had great impact in government circles, and Kennedy followed most of its recommendations.

Kennedy impressed political analysts with the high quality of his appointments to important posts, and his approach to the SEC was no exception. To head the agency he chose William L. Cary, a professor of law at Columbia University who had previously served as staff lawyer at both the SEC and the Department of Justice. Kennedy also elevated two highly regarded SEC staffers, Manuel Cohen and Philip Loomis, to the status of commissioner. Congress approved the hiring of 250 more employees, and Cary put a great deal of time and effort into finding the best people available. Historian John Brooks described the end result: "The atmosphere at the tarpaper shack soon changed from one of bureaucratic somnolence to one of academic liberal activism."

The SEC found that it was not easy to plunge in again after 20 years on the sidelines. It was necessary, above all, to understand exactly what had been happening to the securities markets. To provide the agency with a basis for action, Congress appropriated $750,000 for a massive SEC study. Published in 1963, this document, *The Report of Special Study of Securities Markets*, included the first detailed analysis of stock trading by means of sophisticated computer techniques.

The 1,600-page study revealed that many brokers—particularly in the OTC market—worked on a part-time basis and lacked sufficient knowledge of the markets and of the rules they were supposed to follow. In addition, a substantial number of brokerage firms did not have enough cash in reserve to pay off claims made by investors. The study also uncovered serious abuses in the AMEX, which had been created to deal in the stocks of companies too small to be listed on the NYSE. (In the 1980s a company was required to have pretax earnings of $25 million and 1 million shares of publicly held stock in order to be listed on the NYSE.) The AMEX, which had begun as a tumultuous outdoor exchange, had unfortunately not left behind some of the unsavory practices of the pre-SEC era. Large amounts of stock were sometimes sold without meeting the disclosure rules of the Securities Act, and the AMEX governors allowed certain favored brokers to manipulate stock prices. One of the SEC's major accomplishments in the 1960s was to convince the leaders of Wall Street

William L. Cary, chairman of the SEC from 1961 to 1964, breathed new life into the agency by taking an activist role in regulating the securities industry. He led the SEC's successful effort to reform the American Stock Exchange (AMEX).

that cleaning up the AMEX was in their best interest. The reforms were made, without full-scale government intervention, and the AMEX soon became an important component of the securities industry.

The SEC study also revealed that the floor traders had regained their former position of dominance at the NYSE, holding a majority of the 1,366 seats on the exchange. And the painstaking analysis of stock-trading patterns confirmed once again what the SEC had always maintained: Floor traders, being in the midst of the action, were often able to take advantage of privileged information and were able to manipulate prices for their own benefit. In August 1964, after negotiation with the NYSE, the SEC introduced new rules governing floor traders. Under the rules, a maximum of 30 floor traders would be allowed to operate on the NYSE; the traders would have to possess $250,000 in capital,

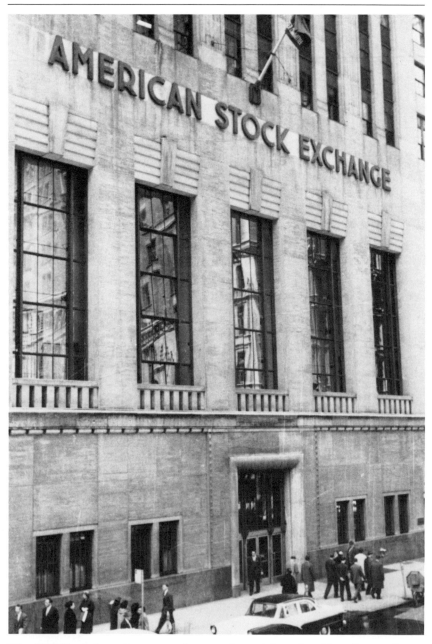

The AMEX originated as an outdoor market, with traders literally standing in the streets or on the curb. It moved indoors in 1921.

would be barred from operating as both brokers and traders in the same session, and would be obliged to make 75 percent of their trades against the price trend (this was meant to prevent traders from purposely driving the price of stocks up or down). These measures reduced the volume of floor trading by 75 percent. But it was a matter of lasting frustration to Cary that he was unable to get rid of the floor traders entirely. Even in reduced numbers they still had a powerful impact on the market, and the SEC recognized that in the rapid fluctuation of stock trading its new rules against price manipulation could easily be circumvented.

Cary had been William O. Douglas's student at Yale, and he sometimes used Douglas's blunt language when talking to business leaders. But he was really closer to Landis in his scholarly and cautious approach to legislation. In a 1980 interview, he expressed his disappointment over the failure to completely reform the NYSE: "We waffled around and wound up with a series of rules that did not achieve much."

Cary also found that Congress was not in the same mood it had been in during the First Hundred Days in 1933. Following the 1963 study, the SEC requested new legislation that would give the agency jurisdiction over more than 2,500 stocks traded on the OTC market. OTC stocks were issued by new companies too small to be listed on either the NYSE or the AMEX, and they were often attractive to investors because of their potential for rapid growth in value. They also were potentially worthless, and the SEC wanted to give investors a better idea of what they were buying.

The proposed law also gave the SEC authority to demand higher capital reserves for investment firms and stricter licensing requirements for brokers, especially in the OTC market. The proposals were all justified by the 1963 study and even had the support of many people on Wall Street. But there was no Sam Rayburn to guide them through Congress—the legendary "Mr. Speaker" had died in 1961. Now the SEC bill was held up in committee month after month as various members of Congress expressed doubts about imposing more regulations on business. Part of the problem was that President Kennedy, after giving the SEC its initial boost, basically lost interest in securities legislation—as in the case of most post–World War II presidents, his real passion was foreign policy. The Securities Act Amendments of 1964 finally got through Congress after 14 and a half months, but many of the original bill's tougher provisions had been pared down.

When Lyndon B. Johnson succeeded to the presidency after the assassination of John F. Kennedy in 1963, he called in the heads of all the regulatory agencies and told them that he wanted cooperation with business rather than control of it. Cary felt that there was nothing more for him to do at the SEC and submitted his resignation. Reflecting on his experiences in a book entitled *Politics and the Regulatory Agencies*, he assessed the position of agencies such as the SEC in the political world: "Without the cooperation of both Congress and the Executive, little constructive can be achieved. To emphasize the point, an agency is literally helpless if either branch is uninterested or unwilling to lend support."

The Go-Go Years and After

Manuel Cohen took over as chairman when William Cary resigned in 1964. He was determined to take an activist role despite President Johnson's warning and Cary's disillusionment. Cohen, a native of Brooklyn, New York, had spent 22 years as an SEC staff attorney before becoming a commissioner. He was so dedicated to the agency and its work and so knowledgeable about SEC operations that people in Washington began calling him "Mr. SEC." As such, Cohen was not disposed to stand by while the SEC was shoved into the background again. "Regulation is not a dirty word," he insisted. "We should not be afraid to regulate."

In 1968, President Lyndon B. Johnson (right) meets with SEC chairman Manuel Cohen, who successfully enforced rules against insider trading and helped establish effective regulation of the mutual funds industry.

Cohen took on an enormous task. In the first place, it was obviously going to be difficult for the SEC to get things done without the support of the White House and Congress. On an operational level, the SEC now had to deal with a securities industry that was growing more and more complex.

In 1960 the NYSE achieved a record when 5.3 million shares of stock were traded in a single day. By 1968 the volume on an *average* day was two and a half times greater. During that same period the total value of NYSE stocks increased from $38 billion to $145 billion. John Brooks had ample reason to entitle his book on this period *The Go-Go Years*. And perhaps the most startling feature of the Go-Go Years was the rise in the number of stockholders—by the end of the 1960s there were 30 million of them. The so-called era of people's capitalism had definitely arrived. Whereas in the 1920s the stock market had still been the preserve of those people able to invest substantial sums, in the 1960s it seemed that every American with a few dollars to spare could buy a piece of American business.

People's capitalism was made possible by the emergence of *mutual funds*. A mutual fund is a company that pools the money of hundreds or thousands of small investors and then trades large amounts of securities representing a wide variety of firms and industries. The mutual fund approach also makes it possible for large institutions such as insurance companies and pension funds to invest huge sums in the stock market without risking their funds on the performance of one stock or a small group of stocks. The emergence of the funds in the 1960s naturally made large amounts of capital available to American business.

But mutual funds also provided opportunities for abuses. Sales commissions, known as loads, were sometimes half the initial investment. And the trading of huge blocks of stock could ultimately destabilize the market and create opportunities for fund managers to manipulate prices.

Finally, the growth of corporate takeovers added to the complexity of the financial scene. In a typical takeover, one company gains control of another by buying up a majority of the target company's stock. This is a bonanza for stockholders of the target company, because the buyer offers a good deal more than the market value of the stock. Typically, the stocks of both companies involved will be heavily traded, producing large commissions for brokers. The law firms and investment banks that devise the takeover strategies and arrange financing also earn multimillion-dollar fees for their services. However, there is also fertile ground here for abuses that ultimately harm investors, such as insider trading (trading by individuals who learn of the impending takeover before the public does) and an inflation of stock values that may lead to heavy losses when prices drop. Economists continually debate whether takeovers benefit the economy or invite disaster.

Chairman Cohen's first priority in meeting these challenges was to bolster the morale of the SEC staff. He pestered the administration and Congress until he got funds for a new SEC building, which was erected at North Capitol and E streets, NW, nearby other government buildings. He also made sure that a give-and-take atmosphere prevailed throughout the agency: Younger staffers were encouraged to approach their superiors whenever they had suggestions or criticisms to offer. Though times had changed, Cohen was clearly trying to revive the energy and idealism of the New Deal years.

Cohen's SEC made headlines in 1965 by bringing a major insider trading case against the Texas Gulf Sulphur Company. The action was taken because executives of Texas Gulf Sulphur had bought stock in their own company when they learned about a huge mineral discovery in Canada that would increase the company's profits. The executives bought their stock before the mineral discovery was announced to the public. As soon as the news broke, people naturally rushed to buy Texas Gulf Sulphur stock: The price of the stock went up, and the executives were able to sell their shares for a considerable profit. The SEC felt this behavior violated the securities laws. In bringing a civil suit against Texas Gulf Sulphur and 13 of its directors, executives, and employees, the SEC was taking its first major action against a large corporation since World War II. It was a hard-fought case, but in 1968 the U.S. Court of Appeals ruled that the defendants had indeed violated the SEC's Rule 10b-5 against insider trading and were obliged to "disgorge" their profits. The judgment established a landmark in securities law enforcement and paved the way for future actions.

The SEC's pursuit of Texas Gulf Sulphur showed an aggressiveness reminiscent of the Douglas years. With respect to the growing rate of corporate takeovers, however, the SEC appeared to prefer the more measured approach favored by James Landis. In October 1965, Senator Harrison Williams of New Jersey introduced a bill requiring any company that desired to buy 5 percent or more of another company's stock to make standard financial disclosures and to announce its intentions 20 days before making any offer. This was designed to give the target company time to mount a defense. Chairman Cohen later indicated that he had wanted even stronger measures than those proposed in the Williams bill. But while the bill was being debated (and delayed) in Congress, the SEC felt constrained by the political atmosphere in Washington to take a neutral position: The agency supported the idea of financial disclosures by the stock buyer but refused to take a stand either for or against takeovers. (The NYSE took the same position.) In 1968, Congress

Townspeople crowded the Timmons, Ontario, stock exchange in 1964 when Texas Gulf Sulphur Co. announced a major mineral strike nearby. The announcement triggered a trading boom of the company's stock. Executives of the company violated insider trading laws by purchasing stock before the announcement.

finally passed the Williams Act in a watered-down version. The waiting period was not adopted, and financial disclosure was required only for offers of 10 percent or more of the target company's stock. A later study indicated that takeovers increased substantially after the passage of the law, possibly because Congress had in effect legitimized the process by setting up a framework for it.

Regulation of mutual funds was perhaps the SEC's primary concern under Cohen. In 1967 the SEC drafted legislation to end all up-front sales charges and to establish a maximum five percent fee for all fund advisers. But many financial experts, economists, and members of Congress strongly objected to the SEC's approach. They argued that fixed rates would stifle competition and make it harder for mutual funds to give investors the services they might want. (The SEC eventually accepted these arguments and in 1975 abolished all fixed commission rates in the securities markets.) Congress finally enacted the suggested revisions of the Investment Company Act in 1970, but in a milder version that called for "reasonable rates" and nothing more. It was a partial victory for Cohen, but by that time he had retired from the SEC.

According to John Brooks, by the fall of 1969 "talent and morale at the SEC had reached rock bottom." The revitalization under Cary and Cohen was over. President Richard M. Nixon, elected in 1968, declared that no new oversight of the securities industry was needed, and he cut the SEC's budget accordingly. His initial appointments to the commission were generally undistinguished. The SEC was reduced to a purely technical function, processing applications from companies wishing to issue new stocks. There was so much activity in the markets, according to Brooks, that "businessmen bringing their applications to the SEC building were being issued numbers to designate their turns, like customers at a crowded meat counter." The SEC charged a fee for processing each application. And thus, according to Brooks, the SEC ended 1969 in the very peculiar position (for a government agency) of showing a profit on its books.

The unbridled trading of the Go-Go Years ended in 1970 with the most devastating collapse of stock prices since 1929. Unlike 1929, though, the markets and the economy were strong enough to survive the shock without a full-scale depression. But a serious business recession followed, and this may have convinced Nixon that stronger direction was needed from the SEC. In 1971 he chose William Casey to be the new chairman of the agency. At first, no one considered this much of a departure, because Casey's main qualification appeared to be his close association with high-ranking Republicans. Although he was a practicing attorney, he was far better known as a swashbuckling

William Casey, a colorful lawyer and securities speculator, served as SEC chairman from 1971 to 1973. He proved less sympathetic to business interests than anticipated and increased the SEC staff by 500 employees.

cloak-and-dagger operative during World War II and as a freewheeling businessman who had made millions in a variety of enterprises. The Senate took a close look at Casey's business dealings but eventually approved him.

In the tradition of Joe Kennedy, Wild Bill Casey turned out to be a much better SEC chairman than anyone expected. He pressured the White House into increasing the SEC's budget requests and added 500 employees to the staff in 3 years. Under Casey's direction the SEC began a concerted effort to abolish fixed commission rates and to create a unified national securities market. Unfortunately, it seemed that Casey could not steer clear of controversy for very long. After being accused of hampering a congressional investigation into Republican party finances, Casey left the SEC in 1973 to take up a post in the State Department. Later he served as director of the Central Intelligence Agency (CIA) in the Reagan administration, and before his death in 1987 he was implicated in the illegal sale of arms to Iran and the diversion of funds to covert U.S. operations in Nicaragua.

Watergate and Its Aftermath

The only political scandal that has ever touched the SEC occurred during the 1973–74 Watergate crisis, when President Nixon and a number of his closest

Robert Vesco is escorted into a Nassau, Bahamas, court to face an extradition hearing in 1973. Vesco had fled the United States to avoid being charged with securities fraud; as of 1989 he had not been extradited to stand trial in the United States.

advisers were accused of engineering and then covering up a burglary of the Democratic party headquarters (housed in Washington's Watergate complex).

In 1973, President Nixon appointed J. Bradford Cook to succeed William Casey as the head of the SEC. At 35 years old—the youngest SEC chairman in history—Cook had a solid legal background and had served as general counsel under Casey. But he never had a chance to demonstrate his abilities. He had barely settled into his office when he was implicated in the web of illegalities and improprieties surrounding the Watergate break-in. According to testimony given in the trial of former attorney general John Mitchell and former commerce secretary Maurice Stans, Cook had agreed to delete from SEC documents all mention of a secret $200,000 contribution to the Republican party by Robert Vesco, a financier who had fled the United States to avoid indictment for securities fraud. Cook was not charged with any crime, but he felt compelled to resign only 74 days after his appointment.

Increasingly preoccupied with the deepening scandal that would eventually force him out of office, President Nixon turned the SEC over to Ray Garrett, Jr., a well-respected securities lawyer from Chicago. Garrett, who had served as a staff attorney at the SEC during the 1950s, encouraged a give-and-take atmosphere within the agency, similar to that which had prevailed under Manuel Cohen. He also ensured the appointment of highly qualified people to the remaining commissioners' posts.

With a top-flight commission behind him and a volatile political climate prevailing in Washington, Garrett was able to achieve considerable independence from the White House. This was evident in the SEC's effort to uncover payments made by U.S. corporations to foreign governments in return for business favors. The congressional investigation into the Watergate scandal had revealed that as many as 450 corporations maintained "slush funds" for the purpose of bribing government officials in foreign countries; contrary to federal law and SEC accounting rules, these payments were concealed in the companies' ledgers. The SEC's work in ferreting out these practices led to the passage of the Foreign Corrupt Practices Act of 1977 and to increased scrutiny of the way corporations are run.

The SEC's concern with corporate governance continued under Roderick Hills, who became chairman of the agency after Richard Nixon resigned in 1974 and was succeeded by Vice-president Gerald Ford. Hills encouraged the SEC's Division of Enforcement, led by Stanley Sporkin, to hunt down unreported corporate contributions to American political parties. One of the SEC's most heralded actions in this area was brought against the American Ship Building Company, owned by George Steinbrenner, who also owned the New York Yankees baseball team. For his role in covering up a large illegal campaign contribution to the Republican party, Steinbrenner received a suspended prison sentence in return for a guilty plea and was also barred from major-league baseball for six months. American Ship Building settled its case with the SEC by agreeing to have a special committee review all its political contributions, and this settlement became the model for many subsequent agreements between the SEC and corporations that wished to avoid formal action.

When Jimmy Carter was elected president in 1976, it might have been expected that, as a liberal Democrat, he would adopt a vigorous approach to securities regulation. Harold Williams, President Carter's choice for SEC chairman, was known as an outspoken critic of the way corporations were being run. He believed that boards of directors, who were supposed to oversee the actions of corporations' chief officers, were often too close to management to be able to do their job. The SEC held extensive hearings on this issue and adopted rules to make corporations more responsive to the views of shareholders. However, neither Carter nor Williams endorsed the idea, proposed by

65

"I built Schwab for investors who want the best of both worlds..."

"Superb service and commission discounts.

Everything we do here at Schwab is designed to make investing easier and more profitable for you.

With our state-of-the-art computer system, we can speed your orders to any major exchange in seconds. We can often confirm your trade while you're still on the phone. And no matter when you call—day or night—you'll have the assistance of a fully-qualified broker who will go out of his or her way to serve you.

For personal assistance, you can visit any of over 100 Schwab offices.

All these services, plus a broad choice of investments are yours *in addition* to the commission discounts we offer on every stock trade. So there's no need to lower your expectations when you want a lower commission.

Just give us a call. We'll send you a free booklet describing all our quality services and discounts."

Charles Schwab
America's Largest Discount Broker

Charles R. Schwab
Chairman

Discount brokers, such as Charles Schwab & Co., Inc., trade securities for customers at a lower commission rate than full-service brokers.

former SEC chairman William Cary and other experts, that the federal government adopt new legislation to revamp the structure of corporate boards.

The most far-reaching achievement of the SEC during the 1970s was the abolition of all fixed commission rates as of May 1, 1975. The SEC had long believed that the fixed commissions charged by brokers for every trade were generally too high and forced many investors to pay for services they did not want. After May Day, as the abolition date became known, the financial services industry was opened up to competition and offered consumers a far greater array of options. Now investors could choose between *discount brokers*, who simply traded stock without providing advice or analysis of the market; *investment advisers*, who offered nothing but analysis; and *full-service brokers*, who offered both trading and advice.

The new arrangement clearly enabled many investors to save money on commissions. It also had consequences that may not have been foreseen, because the sudden competition from discount brokers severely cut into the profits of the large investment firms. To make up the lost revenues, the big firms decided to risk their own money on the markets. This obviously stimulated the markets, but it also meant that large amounts of stock were being traded very aggressively by experts who knew all the tricks of the trade. The stock market of the 1980s became a highly dynamic but ultimately dangerous place in which to do business.

Reaganomics and the SEC

Ronald Reagan entered the White House in 1981 with the stated conviction that business should be free of government restraints. He was convinced that this was the only way to dispel the economic stagnation that had gripped the country during the late 1970s. According to a report in the *New York Times*, a number of Reagan's supporters (some of whom were still attacking Franklin Roosevelt and the New Deal half a century after its inception) were urging the president to all but abolish the SEC. They wanted the agency to give up its regulatory functions and to concentrate on stimulating investment—in other words, to operate as little more than a public relations arm of the securities industry. They also urged Reagan to cut the SEC's budget to the bone.

However, the president-elect's transition team—those advisers given the task of developing the new administration's agenda—concluded from their study of government operations that the SEC was "a model agency." The administration did finally propose budget cuts for the SEC, as for virtually

During John S. R. Shad's tenure as chairman of the SEC (1981–87), the agency increased its pursuit of insider trading violators.

every other area of government except defense, but it did not propose any major revision of the SEC's powers or status. With the Democrats still in control of the House of Representatives, where all money bills originate, it was unlikely in any case that a radical anti-SEC measure would have succeeded. The House did, however, authorize some of the cuts in the agency's staff and budget.

The Senate, although controlled by President Reagan's own party, raised serious objections to President Reagan's choice for SEC chairman, John S. R. Shad. Shad had been a high-ranking executive in the investment firm of E. F. Hutton and thus was expected to be an opponent of strict regulation. He was also very wealthy in his own right. After looking closely at some of Shad's personal business dealings, the Senate finally approved his appointment.

Shad apparently agreed with the Reagan policy of relaxing restrictions on business. He informed corporations that they would not be required to reveal as much negative information about their financial position as in the past, and he advised them to emphasize the positive. He scrapped a computer system that had just been developed for the analysis of stock trading. He allowed companies to file a single form for all the securities they expected to issue over a two-year period rather than the separate forms that had been required for each individual issue. (This new rule saved companies millions of dollars in administrative costs.) Finally, Shad lowered the requirement for the amount of capital that investment firms had to have backing up their stock trades.

The SEC's new approach undoubtedly contributed to the expansion of the markets and the growth of new capital. The *New York Times* estimated in 1983 that the SEC moves had brought another $500 million into the markets. At the same time, the Reagan administration sponsored a massive tax cut that left corporations with large amounts of extra money on hand. In theory, the money would be used to create more goods and more jobs, but in many cases it was used to take over other companies. This, too, was good for the markets. Wall Street, which had seen some hard times since the 1970 slump, began to boom. New buildings were going up throughout the financial district in lower Manhattan, and firms were hiring thousands of new workers. Suddenly Wall Street was the place to be for the energetic and the ambitious: The most successful bankers and traders found huge bonuses in their Christmas envelopes, and specialists in takeover maneuvers could amass fortunes in a matter of months with a few shrewd gambles. All this activity clearly bolstered the economy in the short run. But some students of the financial scene, such as the prominent investment banker Felix Rohatyn of Lazard Frères &

Investment banker Felix Rohatyn raised a voice of caution during the bull market of the mid-1980s.

Company publicly condemned the "Jazz Age mentality" prevailing on Wall Street. And many state officials responsible for securities regulation complained that the SEC was not doing enough to protect investors from the pitfalls that every booming market inevitably contains.

Chairman Shad replied that the SEC was "just as vigilant as we've always been in requiring proper disclosures, but not in the degree of detail—unless they're material—and that's our standard." Although he had initially acceded to the administration's budget-cutting fervor, once installed as chairman, Shad fought against any further reductions in the SEC budget and succeeded in holding the line. He had also vowed when taking office to come down "with hobnail boots" on anyone guilty of insider trading. This statement boosted the morale of SEC staffers, and it appears that they never forgot it. When Shad retired in 1987, they presented him with a pair of hobnail boots.

More significantly, the SEC made good on Shad's promise. Between 1934 and 1981, the agency had brought only 50 complaints for insider trading violations, the most prominent being the Texas Gulf Sulphur case. Between 1981 and 1986, in contrast, the agency pursued another 50 cases. One of them involved Paul Thayer, a former Defense Department official who had entered the business world. In 1984 the SEC accused Thayer of passing inside information while an officer of two different corporations: Eventually he pleaded guilty to criminal charges, surrendered $850,000 in illegal profits, and received a 4-year prison sentence. The SEC also pursued actions against the prestigious investment banking firm of Kidder, Peabody & Company, which was charged with mishandling customers' funds and with insider trading. In a foretaste of the more spectacular Drexel Burnham case, Kidder, Peabody settled the complaint out of court. The company gave up $13.7 million in profits, paid a penalty of $11.6 million, and agreed to restructure its management. So the SEC could certainly not be accused, in this area, of going easy on the rich and the well connected.

The most spectacular of all the insider cases, and unquestionably the most far-reaching the SEC has ever instituted, began in 1985. Dennis Levine, an investment banker with the firm of Drexel Burnham Lambert Inc., had established a bank account in the Bahamas. Through this account he traded stocks based on inside information he received from accomplices in law firms and other banks, who knew when takeovers were in the offing. SEC investigation HO-1743, which finally exposed Levine, was a complicated operation. The SEC had to trace trades spanning 6 years and worth almost $100 million in the stock of 114 different companies. (Levine had made a profit of almost $12 million.) It had to establish that there was a pattern to the trades—that each purchase had uncannily preceded a takeover bid that increased the value of the stock. Then the SEC had to convince the bank, a Swiss firm operating outside the jurisdiction of the U.S. government, to reveal that the "Mr. Diamond" who owned the account was in fact Dennis B. Levine of 225 East 57th Street in New York City. When the SEC closed in on Levine and his confederates in the spring of 1986, Levine revealed that he himself had passed information to Ivan Boesky, one of Wall Street's leading speculators in takeover stocks. Boesky, in turn, implicated Drexel Burnham Lambert as well as its leading specialist in high-yield corporate bonds, Michael Milken.

The Levine-Boesky case greatly enhanced the agency's reputation as the scourge of Wall Street criminals. But even as they praised the SEC's investigative work, some members of Congress were outraged that the agency had allowed Boesky to sell off some $400 million in personal stock holdings before his indictment was publicly announced. The objection was that even

A grim-faced Ivan Boesky (second from left) leaves court in December 1987 after pleading guilty to a charge of filing false information with the SEC. He received a three-year prison sentence. In 1986, Boesky had agreed to the SEC's demand that he pay a $100 million fine to settle the charges of insider trading.

David S. Ruder, SEC chairman from 1987 to 1989, testifies before a Senate committee hearing to review recent developments in the securities markets.

though Boesky eventually had to pay a $100-million fine and serve a prison sentence of 3 years, the gradual sale of his stock enabled him to make a greater profit than he deserved. In defending its action, the SEC cited the possibility that the sudden dumping off of such a large amount of stock would have caused a catastrophic drop in the market. In light of the crash on October 19, 1987, the SEC's fears were not at all unreasonable.

David S. Ruder, a Chicago securities attorney and dean of the Northwestern University Law School, had already succeeded John Shad as chairman when the crash occurred, and he had the difficult task of trying to restore order to the markets and prevent further shocks. *Business Week* magazine entitled its story on Ruder's appointment THE ODD MAN OUT IN REAGAN'S WASHINGTON. Ruder was "odd" because his background was similar to that of most SEC chairmen in the past, whereas the great majority of high officials in the Reagan administration were either former business executives or longtime political associates of the president. *Business Week* conveyed the opinion of Washington insiders that

Ruder lacked the toughness and political savvy necessary to get things done when the administration was insisting that everything was fine on Wall Street, crash or no crash. However, the magazine soon announced that Ruder had become the most persuasive advocate to be found in official Washington and that he had developed a broad base of support for the SEC in Congress. Arguing that the SEC was a "peanut agency doing a giant job," Ruder succeeded in getting the SEC's budget increased.

In the summer of 1988, Ruder sent Congress a wide-ranging set of legislative proposals that would, if passed, greatly increase the authority of the SEC over the operation of the securities markets. At the same time, he indicated a willingness to relax certain restrictions in the interest of stimulating the markets. In effect, Ruder was suggesting that neither the iron-fisted nor the kid-glove method of regulation was sufficient in itself. The size and complexity of the markets appeared to call for a more flexible approach in which competing needs could be balanced. This position may also have reflected differences between the SEC commissioners—it was known that a number of decisions had been made on the basis of a narrow 3–2 vote.

When President George Bush entered the White House in 1989, he did not take any immediate position with regard to the securities markets, though political commentators were convinced that he would be in favor of more regulation than his predecessor was. Nevertheless, Chairman Ruder announced in May 1989 that he was returning to Northwestern University Law School. Even though his term was not due to expire until 1992, he expressed his belief that the new president ought to be able to choose his own SEC head. (Whether the administration's cutting of $8 million from the SEC's budget request played a part in Ruder's decision is open to speculation.) At the same time, Gary Lynch, the director of the Division of Enforcement and the architect of the Levine, Boesky, and Drexel Burnham investigations, submitted his resignation in order to enter private law practice. Thus, the direction to be taken by the SEC during the 1990s became a matter of intense discussion among those who follow the financial scene. Reflecting upon the headline-making enforcement actions of the late 1980s, the *New York Times*, for its part, concluded that Ruder and Lynch were leaving the SEC "at its zenith in terms of public confidence."

The SEC building at 405 Fifth Street, NW, in Washington, D.C.

FOUR

Regulating the Securities Markets

As an independent regulatory agency, the SEC belongs to what has traditionally been called the fourth branch of the U.S. government. The Constitution provided for only three branches—the executive, the legislative, and the judicial—but the regulatory agencies came into being to meet specific needs and have become a permanent feature of political life in America. Like high-ranking members of the executive branch, the five commissioners who direct the SEC are appointed by the president with the approval of the Senate. One commissioner is specifically appointed to serve as chairman. Once sworn in, the commissioners cannot be dismissed by the president before the expiration of their five-year term. In addition, the terms are staggered so that no more than one commissioner will retire in any given year; this is intended to ensure continuity in the policies of the SEC. And according to the provisions of the Securities Exchange Act of 1934, no more than three of the commissioners can belong to the same political party. Thus, a Democratic president may have to appoint a Republican to the SEC, and vice versa. All policy decisions are decided by a majority vote of the commissioners.

Critics of the SEC—and of other regulatory agencies, such as the Federal Aviation Administration, the Nuclear Regulatory Commission, the FDA, the Environmental Protection Agency, and the Federal Communications

75

Commission—have often objected that democratic principles are violated when power is given to people who have not been selected by the voters. This is not an argument that can be brushed aside. But defenders of the agencies point out that in matters as important as nuclear energy, public health, civil aviation, securities trading, and the like, it is essential to rely on a corps of professionals who are committed to act in the public interest. They argue that this ideal can be better achieved when policymakers do not have to tailor their views to the popular ideas or political fashions of the moment, which may or may not be beneficial to the country in the long run.

The SEC is directly responsible to Congress. Although the executive branch submits the annual budget request for the agency, Congress decides on the amount of the appropriation. The SEC submits an annual report to Congress and special reports on specific subjects when requested to do so. Despite its independence from presidential control, in practice it has often been difficult for the SEC and other agencies to get needed funds and legislation from Congress without strong support from the White House. Thus, the president is able to exert considerable influence on regulatory policy.

Despite the antiregulatory climate of the 1980s, the position of the SEC and the other regulatory agencies was not seriously shaken. In the case of the SEC, even critics of its policies over the years have usually conceded that it is the best-organized and most effective agency in Washington. It is impressive to consider that although the size and complexity of the securities markets have increased dramatically since the creation of the SEC, the agency is doing its work with slightly more than 2,000 employees, only 400 more than it had half a century ago. The high quality of its staff and the basic procedures established during the New Deal years, along with the aid of computers, enable the SEC to operate efficiently.

The SEC is organized into four principal divisions, plus supporting offices. Each division is headed by a director appointed by the chairman, frequently but not necessarily from the ranks of the SEC staff. The divisions of the SEC are the Division of Corporation Finance, the Division of Enforcement, the Division of Market Regulation, and the Division of Investment Management.

The Division of Corporation Finance

The Division of Corporation Finance ensures that corporations satisfy all the disclosure requirements established by the Securities Act of 1933. This involves registration and analysis of all new stock offerings and of the quarterly

Companies publish annual reports to inform investors of company performance during the preceding fiscal year.

and annual reports, known respectively as 10-Qs and 10-Ks, submitted to the SEC by all corporations whose stock is held by the public. If, on the other hand, a company proposes to sell its stock only to persons with "sufficient" business experience and knowledge of the company—such as the company's officers— the SEC considers this to be a *private offering* and does not require disclosure. Stocks sold exclusively within a single state are also exempt from federal disclosure regulations but are subject to the requirements of state law. The SEC also allows exemptions for some small businesses wishing to sell stock and provides others with simplified methods of reporting data. The Division of Corporation Finance maintains an Office of Small Business Policy to provide assistance in this area.

The purpose of the disclosure rules is simple. In order for an investor to make a sensible decision about buying the stock of a certain company, the investor needs to know how the company is doing. It is not enough to be told that the company is large, well established, and making a profit. In deciding whether or not a company's stock is likely to rise in value, an investor might want to know how much the company has invested in research and new equipment, how much money it owes to banks and bond holders, whether its

Certified public accountants (CPAs) must pass a rigorous examination and meet state requirements in order to practice public accounting. The SEC's Office of the Chief Accountant issues Accounting Series Releases (ASRs) to help keep accountants up-to-date on the correct methods of reporting corporate financial information.

earnings have gone up or down in recent years, and a number of other facts. All this information is contained in the 10-Qs and 10-Ks. These reports are available to the public in a number of SEC offices and in many public libraries.

Under the Securities Exchange Act, each stockholder in a company must receive an annual report within 90 days of the end of the fiscal year. Large corporations may spend several hundred thousand dollars to produce impressive reports, complete with color photographs and sophisticated charts. Behind the optimistic message from the chairman of the board and the essays on the company's activities come pages of financial information—not as detailed as the 10-Qs and 10-Ks, but enough to present a clear picture of the company's financial position.

Each year the SEC receives 11 million pages of disclosure data from corporations. Even with the use of computers, verification of this data might well require all the agency's 2,000 employees and more—if not for an important decision made when the SEC was created. In order to avoid the creation of a huge staff, Cohen, Corcoran, and Landis decided to let certified public accountants—those who have met the requirements of state law and have been licensed to practice—confirm the accuracy of the financial data. Anyone who studies an annual report will see, after all the numbers are presented, a letter from an independent accounting firm. The accountants verify that they have reviewed the information in the report and have found that it accurately represents the financial condition of the company. The work of the accountants is reviewed by the SEC's Office of the Chief Accountant, and the accountants are subject to penalties for any violations of SEC accounting procedures. The companies themselves are responsible for providing truthful information to the accountants.

Whenever a company decides to issue a new security, it files a registration statement containing the disclosure data with the SEC. The SEC makes this information public as soon as it is received, but the stock cannot be sold at once. There is a 20-day "cooling-off period," during which time the SEC reviews the data to make sure that it is complete. The SEC may send a "letter of comment" to the underwriters of the stock indicating how the registration statement needs to be improved. Once the improvements are made, the SEC formally accepts the registration statement. Then the underwriters send a formal prospectus to potential investors, and the stock is on the market. If, however, the SEC finds serious deficiencies in the registration statement, it can suspend the sale of the stock by issuing a *stop order*.

A Long Island Railroad Company stock certificate representing ownership of 60,000 shares of the company's stock. Before a company issues stock it must file a registration statement, including financial dislosures, with the SEC.

The stop order is perhaps the most effective single weapon at the SEC's command. The threat of a legal case that will take months, or even years, to decide may not deter unscrupulous issuers from violating disclosure laws. While the case is going through the courts, the public may have been defrauded, and the offenders, if they can be found, may be willing to forfeit part of their illegal profits in the form of a fine. The stop order, by contrast, ensures that no damage will be done in the first place. Experience has shown that the very threat of a stop order—upsetting the timing of the sale and causing the stock to appear suspicious in the eyes of investors—is enough to ensure compliance with the disclosure rules. By adopting what lawyers call a "licensing" approach to regulation rather than a "punitive" approach, the SEC has been able to protect investors in the most efficient possible manner.

It is important to emphasize, however, that the SEC does not give advice on the soundness of an investment or guarantee that investors will make money by buying stocks approved by the agency. The SEC only certifies that the sellers of the stock have given the public the means to make an intelligent decision. If that decision does not turn out to be profitable, it will be a waste of time complaining to the SEC except in cases of fraud.

The Division of Enforcement

The Division of Enforcement has earned much publicity during the 1980s as a result of its insider trading investigations. The public impression may be that enforcement is the major activity of the SEC and that insider trading is the major thrust of enforcement. In fact, the Division of Enforcement does have approximately 650 employees, almost one-third of the agency's total. But according to figures released in 1989, the Division of Enforcement devotes only 15 percent of its resources to insider trading cases. Cases involving market manipulation and improper disclosures actually receive more attention. Thus, it was a relatively small group of investigators who, within a year's time, untangled all the complex elements of Dennis Levine's insider trading scheme and built the case against him and his associates. This accomplishment demonstrates the talent and tenacity of the SEC investigators.

In the enforcement area, too, the SEC relies to some extent on the self-interest and self-regulation of the securities industry. The Levine case really started when the brokerage firm of Merrill Lynch & Company received an anonymous letter from Venezuela concerning suspicious transactions made through South American banks on a Merrill Lynch account. Merrill Lynch's security staff began its own investigation and then turned over its findings, which proved to be very significant, to the SEC. The NYSE also has a large security staff that monitors all the trading done on the NYSE floor, and the NYSE immediately notifies the SEC whenever a pattern emerges that might suggest insider trading. All other exchanges follow the same procedure.

The SEC's complaints against violators are prepared with great thoroughness. During the mid-1970s sociologist Susan Shapiro, then completing her Ph.D. at Yale University, was given an unprecedented opportunity to study the inner workings of the SEC. She reviewed records not available to the public, observed and interviewed staff members, and sat in on meetings at which major policy decisions were made. Shapiro found that the average investigation took three months, though some had been in progress for as long as four years. In a majority of the cases she studied, the SEC allowed the violators to correct the offenses without formal charges or else referred the question of punishment to a "self-regulatory body," such as the NYSE. On more serious violations the SEC took direct action, with the commissioners making the final decision whether to pursue enforcement. During the time of Shapiro's study the commissioners spent several hours each day reviewing reports of investigations and discussing them with staff members: "The degree of attention given to the minutiae of the individual case and the pertinent evidence was truly impressive," Shapiro observed. "An entire morning might be spent scrutinizing stock market trading data or the accounting work papers pertaining to a single offense. . . . Determinations pertaining to all aspects of a given case often continued over days, weeks, or months."

If the commissioners decide that direct action by the SEC is called for, the offender may be summoned for a hearing at the SEC, to be conducted by an administrative law judge (administrative law judges are civil servants who conduct hearings for regulatory agencies). The hearing may be public or private, according to the discretion of the SEC, and it must follow the requirements of the federal laws for due process of law and fairness to defendants. The decision of the administrative law judge is subject to review by the commissioners, who may either accept it or decide that further action is necessary. In most cases, a settlement is reached at the hearing stage. Typically, the defendant will agree to a penalty (surrendering the profits from a stock trade, for example) without either admitting or denying any wrongdoing.

In more complicated cases, the SEC will institute full-scale civil proceedings in the federal district courts. Those who are found guilty of violating the securities laws can be ordered to pay a substantial cash penalty. The courts may also give the SEC authority to reorganize a firm's operations in order to end improper practices. In Susan Shapiro's survey of several hundred cases, 91 percent of the civil suits and 89 percent of the administrative hearings were decided in favor of the SEC.

The SEC does not prosecute anyone for criminal offenses. In cases such as those involving Dennis Levine and Ivan Boesky, where there appears to be criminal activity such as fraud and conspiracy, the SEC will turn its information over to the Department of Justice, and a U.S. attorney will seek criminal indictments. In the case against Drexel Burnham Lambert Inc., a complicated chain of events unfolded. First, the SEC decided to delay its civil lawsuit against the firm until after the Justice Department pursued criminal charges because the prosecutors wanted to avoid revealing some of their evidence in a civil trial. Then the Justice Department decided to accept a guilty plea from Drexel Burnham, on the condition that the firm pay a $650 million fine, work out an agreement with the SEC, and submit to the SEC's penalties. The settlement, formally approved by the federal courts in June 1989, concluded the largest securities-fraud action in the SEC's history. In addition to

Michael Milken, head of the "junk bond" division of Drexel Burnham Lambert Inc., leaves federal court in New York in April 1989 after pleading innocent to charges of insider trading. The SEC's information about Milken's activities was essential to the Justice Department's prosecution of the case.

dismissing Michael Milken, Drexel Burnham agreed to transfer Milken's highly profitable "junk bond" operation from California to New York, where all the firm's operations were to be overseen by the SEC for a three-year period.

As a footnote to the settlement, though not in any way part of it, Drexel Burnham hired former SEC chairman John Shad as chairman of the company and also named Roderick Hills, another retired SEC chairman, and Ralph Saul, formerly a top SEC official as well as a past president of the AMEX, to serve on the company's board of directors. An admitted attempt by Drexel Burnham to reassure clients about the honesty and stability of the firm, these appointments demonstrate the SEC's stature on Wall Street and in the mind of the public.

The Division of Market Regulation

Both the Securities Exchange Act of 1934 and the Investment Advisers Act of 1940 give the SEC authority over the operation of the securities markets and over the conduct of all those engaged in the trading of securities. Over the years, a considerable number of brokers have been suspended by the SEC for violating the rules, and some have been barred for life from selling securities. Complaints about brokers are taken up by the Division of Market Regulation, often after investigation by the Office of Consumer Affairs and Information Services. Each year during the mid-1980s, an average of 45 individuals were suspended from trading in the securities markets for varying periods of time, and another 45 were barred for life.

When it comes to disciplining brokers, the SEC has absolute and final authority, subject only to review by the federal courts when a decision is appealed. The agency does not have to work through the stock exchange or explain its reasons for punishing an exchange member. Furthermore, SEC investigators have the right to enter the offices of brokers and inspect their records at any time, without any need for a court order or even a formal notice. Brokers know that they are directly accountable to the SEC for every trade they make. Here again, the SEC uses the licensing approach to great effect: The threat of being immediately barred from earning a living is much more of a deterrent to a potential violator than a lawsuit that could take years to be decided.

The Division of Market Regulation conducted the SEC probe into the 1987 crash and supervised the publication in 1988 of an 847-page report on the causes underlying the crisis. The division carefully analyzed all of the trades

Panic overtakes the "pit" at the Chicago Board Options Exchange as the market plummets on Black Monday, 1987. The SEC's Division of Market Regulation conducted an investigation into the causes of the crash.

made during the collapse of stock prices. It also interviewed hundreds of brokers and traders and disciplined those whose actions during the crash fell short of SEC standards. The SEC found that a number of "specialist" firms, which have exclusive privileges to handle trades in individual stocks, allowed prices to keep falling even though they are pledged to begin buying with their own funds when the market gets too low. (A number of specialist firms that obeyed the rules were all but wiped out in the crash.) The offending specialists had their trading privileges suspended for varying amounts of time. The SEC also accused Salomon Brothers Inc., a large Wall Street firm, of short selling $12.5 million of stock during the crash. The complaint was settled in May 1989 when Salomon agreed to a semiannual review of all its short sales, without either admitting or denying guilt.

Market regulation is one area in which the philosophical approach of the SEC has resulted in frustration for the agency. Because the securities exchanges are allowed to make their own rules, it is difficult for the SEC to bring about reforms unless the exchanges agree to them. If the exchanges resist the SEC, the only recourse is to get new laws passed by Congress—a difficult task when there is strong opposition from the business community. The SEC has never repeated William Douglas's threat to take over the stock exchange—it is quite obvious to everyone that the SEC has neither the resources nor the backing for such a drastic move.

Sometimes the SEC uses indirect means to bring about changes. The fight over floor trading during the 1960s is a good example. The SEC could not persuade the NYSE to abolish floor trading, but it still had the authority to establish standards for all securities professionals. So the agency announced that the floor traders would have to take a qualifying exam on NYSE and SEC regulations and make daily reports of all the trades they conducted. John Brooks described the effect this rule had on the floor traders: "'They sat us down with a pencil and a glass of water right in the Board of Governors room,' a floor trader cried in outrage. 'Our seats were even spaced far apart, so we couldn't crib!' Shortly after imposition of the new rules, the number of floor traders on the Exchange floor dropped from three hundred to thirty." Even though Chairman William L. Cary was disappointed with this partial solution, it showed how the SEC can make creative use of its broad rule-making powers.

The Division of Investment Management

The Division of Investment Management is responsible for overseeing the management of all mutual funds and investment advisers, under authority granted by Congress in 1940. Because mutual funds have drawn many millions of small investors into the markets, their operations merit careful scrutiny.

On the whole, the SEC has not uncovered serious abuses in mutual funds. In the late 1980s the agency reported that only four percent of the complaints received from investors related to their experience with mutual funds. This speaks well for the management of the funds, but it also says a good deal about the effectiveness of the SEC's oversight. It may be instructive to compare the state of mutual funds with that of the nation's savings and loan institutions, which were freed from government restrictions by the Reagan administration. While mutual funds were flourishing, many of the savings and loan institutions made unwise or dishonest use of their depositors' money. By 1989 the savings and loan industry was in a shambles, and the government had to come up with $100 billion to compensate depositors for their losses.

The Division of Investment Management is also responsible for administering the Public Utility Holding Company Act of 1935. This is one of the most important areas of SEC activity and may be the function that is least

Prospectuses for a wide range of mutual funds are available at Fidelity Investments' walk-in service centers. The SEC's Office of Consumer Affairs and Information Services receives relatively few complaints from investors about mutual funds.

appreciated by the public. At the time of the New Deal, more than half the stock of all the gas and electric companies in the United States was owned by three giant holding companies. A *holding company* is a company that is created for the sole purpose of controlling and trading the stock of other companies. As William O. Douglas recalled in his autobiography: "The holding company in the utility field had become a monster, bleeding [local] operating companies, selling stocks at fantastic prices, living only for the benefit of a few insiders and the investment brokers who serviced them."

In this area the SEC did not rely on the philosophy of self-regulation. The Public Utility Holding Company Act of 1935 gave the SEC the authority to break up the holding companies, and the agency required them to register without delay. The holding companies, realizing that their very existence was at stake, defied the SEC order and hired a battery of top-flight lawyers to plead their case in the federal courts. Finally, in 1938, the U.S. Supreme Court ruled in *Electric Bond and Share v. SEC* that the SEC did have the authority under the Constitution to regulate public utility holding companies. As soon as the decision was handed down, the SEC registered the holding companies and broke them down into a regional system that would be responsive to the needs of individual communities.

Currently, 13 regional holding companies are operating in the utilities field, and all of them are registered with the SEC. The SEC requires that each company be limited to a defined region and that it be small enough to ensure efficient operation. The SEC also enforces strict rules for the buying and selling of securities by holding companies. The purpose of these rules is to prevent losses that would weaken the companies, injure investors, and ultimately result in bigger bills for utility customers. In the judgment of Joel Seligman, the SEC's work in this area has been its most useful accomplishment. Certainly it has been the accomplishment that most affects the average citizen, who may or may not be a stockholder but is almost certainly a customer of a utility company.

Until 1935, holding companies dominated ownership of many public utilities, such as this power plant in Deepwater, N.J. The SEC was authorized by law to split up these holding companies and force them to operate in the public interest.

Offices of the SEC

A number of offices within the commission support and supplement the activities of the four SEC divisions. Among these offices are the Office of the General Counsel, the Office of the Chief Accountant, the Office of Consumer Affairs and Information Services, the Office of Economic Analysis, and the Office of EDGAR Management.

Office of the General Counsel

The Office of the General Counsel is, in effect, the SEC's lawyer. The office, with a staff of approximately 75, reviews all matters relating to the legality of SEC rulings. The Office of the General Counsel also supervises the legal actions that the SEC brings against violators and responds to any legal challenges brought against the agency. In an average year, the Office of the General Counsel prepares as many as 300 cases.

The office's most important function for investors comes into force under Chapter 11 of the U.S. Bankruptcy Code. Under Chapter 11, a company unable to pay its debts can reorganize under court supervision and remain in business while it arranges to pay off its creditors. The bankruptcy code allows the SEC to participate in this procedure whenever the agency believes that the interests of investors or the integrity of a company's securities are at stake. The Office of the General Counsel handles all of the SEC's work in this area.

Office of the Chief Accountant

The Office of the Chief Accountant sets the standards for reporting corporate financial information. The upgrading of accounting procedures has been one of the enduring contributions of the SEC. Prior to the 1930s, accountants were virtually servants of the companies that hired them. If a company wanted to impress potential investors, it merely ordered an accountant to juggle the figures, turning losses into profits. The accountant's only choice was to follow orders or be replaced by a more pliable employee.

One of the principal goals of James M. Landis when he became chairman of the SEC was to enlist accountants in the cause of accurate reporting. According to Professor Thomas McCraw of the Harvard Business School, the accounting profession reacted at first with hostility, objecting to the severe penalties the SEC proposed for those who failed to comply. But after considerable urging by Landis, the accountants realized that the SEC was offering them a chance to upgrade their profession.

Auditing the accounts of businesses is one of the principal activities of CPAs. Investors will more readily trust a company's financial statement if it is accompanied by a report made by an independent accountant.

The Office of the Chief Accountant was created in 1937. It began to issue a series of documents known as Accounting Series Releases (ASRs). These documents keep accountants up-to-date on the proper methods of reporting corporate financial information. The updates are important because revisions of the tax laws often change the rules for calculating different types of income, claiming business losses, and so on. Since 1937 the SEC has issued more than 300 ASRs. In the view of Thomas McCraw, the ASRs have done the accounting profession nothing but good: "[The accounting profession] increased by 271 percent between 1930 and 1970, compared with 73 percent for physicians and 71 percent for lawyers. Small wonder that accountants cooperated enthusiastically with the SEC."

Office of Consumer Affairs and Information Services

The Office of Consumer Affairs and Information Services is the branch of the SEC that deals directly with the public. Whenever an investor makes a complaint to the SEC, the Office of Consumer Affairs investigates the complaint and requests a written reply from all the parties involved. If the Office of Consumer Affairs believes that the securities laws have been violated, it will refer the complaint to the appropriate SEC division for further action. For

A broker phones a client to discuss a potential trade. The SEC will investigate a broker's actions when an investor files a complaint accusing the broker of misconduct.

example, in the case of an errant broker the Division of Market Regulation might impose a suspension, or the Division of Enforcement might decide that a lawsuit is in order. Approximately 25 percent of the SEC's enforcement actions against brokers and securities firms originate in complaints made by investors. In some cases, the SEC and a violator may reach an agreement that includes repayment to investors of any money they have lost, but the SEC never collects money for dissatisfied investors.

During the late 1980s the Office of Consumer Affairs processed an average of 30,000 complaints each year. In 1987, however, the number of complaints jumped to 40,000. During the 6 weeks following the October 19 stock market crash, the SEC received more than 14,000 telephone calls and 1,300 letters from investors unhappy with the way their brokers had performed during the crisis. The SEC found that in many cases the market was so chaotic that brokers could not make trades exactly when customers wanted them made. Other brokers were so overwhelmed by the crash, or so busy trying to save their own investments, that they simply refused to talk to customers on the telephone.

The Office of Applications and Reports Services also maintains a reference service for investors in the SEC's Washington headquarters and in the New York and Chicago regional offices. There, investors can study corporate disclosure statements and other documents related to the securities laws and SEC operations. For investors who cannot come to the reference centers, the office provides copies of documents upon payment of a copying charge.

Office of Economic Analysis

The Office of Economic Analysis, headed by the chief economist, is responsible for the SEC's computer-based studies of the securities markets and the general economy. The Office of Economic Analysis channels the data from these studies to the appropriate divisions and to the commissioners in order to provide an informed basis for their decisions.

Whenever the SEC makes a rule change, such as the 1982 decision allowing companies to file a single form for two years' worth of securities issues, the Office of Economic Analysis conducts a careful study to see what effect the rule may be having on the markets. This allows the SEC to evaluate its own decisions and to revise them when necessary.

Office of EDGAR Management

EDGAR is the Electronic Data Gathering Analysis and Retrieval system being developed by the SEC. In 1984 the agency began a pilot project to develop a computer system capable of handling the 11 million pages of disclosure data received by the agency each year. The goal of the system is to shorten the time it takes to make all this information available to the public and the financial community. When the SEC became convinced in 1987 that a new computer system would be feasible, it created the Office of EDGAR Management to oversee the project.

In 1989 the Office of EDGAR Management awarded a $52 million contract to a group of computer companies that will make the EDGAR system fully operational by 1993. At that time every firm making disclosures to the SEC will be able to transmit the necessary data from its own computers directly into the SEC computers. The SEC computers will then transmit the data by electronic means to anyone wishing to use it. All the details of the system have not been announced, but after 1993 it should be possible for anyone owning a personal computer and the proper software to call up financial data on any corporation filing with the SEC.

Regional Offices of the SEC

The SEC maintains nine regional offices, each one situated in a city where there is significant business activity. The regional offices are located in New York, Boston, Atlanta, Chicago, Fort Worth, Denver, Los Angeles, Seattle, and Philadelphia. There are also smaller regional branch offices in Miami, Houston, Salt Lake City, and San Francisco. A regional administrator, who is appointed by the chairman of the SEC, heads each regional office.

91

The regional offices monitor the activities of the exchanges in their respective locations. They conduct local investigations when necessary and provide information services for investors. The regional offices also offer guidance to owners of small businesses who are interested in making public stock offerings.

The SEC does not issue detailed statistics on the activities of the regional offices. However, Susan Shapiro's study in the mid-1970s concluded that the bulk of the SEC's enforcement work is carried out by the regional offices. General information issued by the SEC would appear to bear this out: The telephone directory for the SEC headquarters in Washington lists slightly more than 200 individuals attached to the Division of Enforcement, which would leave more than 400 to be divided among the regional offices. Such a distribution of personnel would naturally enable the SEC to be more responsive to the needs of businesses and investors in a particular area and also to learn more quickly of any violations. Clearly the greatest danger to investors does not come from formal offerings of stock in leading companies, made by established brokerage firms. The danger comes from a salesman on the telephone representing an unknown company and offering stock in an equally unknown company that—according to the salesman—is about to do great things and provide fabulous returns for investors. Such sales pitches may be legitimate opportunities to invest in new stocks with genuine growth potential,

Trainees practice trading on the floor of the New York Futures Exchange, a small exchange that began operating in 1980. By watching over the smaller securities exchanges in their particular areas, the SEC's 13 regional offices provide investors with further protection.

The seal of the SEC features the shield of the United States. The eagle bears an olive branch (symbolizing peace) and arrows (symbolizing war).

or they may be out-and-out frauds. In the latter case the SEC's regional offices, with their local contacts, would be likely to discover the problem more quickly than the headquarters staff in Washington. They also would have a better chance of stepping in before a large number of people invested money in worthless stock.

The SEC describes its staff as consisting of "lawyers, accountants, financial analysts and examiners, engineers, investigators, economists, and other professionals." The impression conveyed by Susan Shapiro from her inside view of the agency is that SEC attorneys in particular tend to be young and highly dedicated. She found them typically working late into the evening and going home long after the lights had been turned out in other government buildings. However, Shapiro concluded that many of the young attorneys were planning to stay at the SEC a relatively short time before going into private law practice.

The historical record would suggest, not surprisingly, that SEC staffers tend to stay longer when the agency is ably led and highly active. In periods of decline, many of the most able staffers have left the agency to find more challenging work. In any event, the SEC's reputation as the best of the regulatory agencies is undoubtedly due in large part to the quality of the employees it has always managed to attract.

In 1985 stockbroker Peter Brant was sentenced to 8 months in prison and fined $10,000 for trading stocks using insider information about forthcoming Wall Street Journal articles. Congress strengthened the SEC's enforcement powers in 1988 when it passed the Insider Trading and Securities Fraud Enforcement Act, which imposed a jail sentence of up to 10 years and a fine of $1 million per violation.

FIVE

The SEC and the Markets of the Future

As the securities markets grow and diversify, the job of regulation will certainly not become easier. To cope with the broader issues, the SEC is preparing new approaches to such major concerns as insider trading and market regulation. Technologically, the EDGAR system will help the SEC to keep pace.

Insider Trading

In October 1988, Congress passed the Insider Trading and Securities Fraud Enforcement Act. Under this law, those found guilty of insider trading would face a jail sentence of up to 10 years per violation and a fine of $1 million per violation. (Previously, the maximum penalties were 5 years in jail and a $100,000 fine.) Congress raised the fine for securities firms from $500,000 to $2.5 million per violation and stipulated that firms "knowingly or recklessly" failing to supervise employees who violated the law would be liable for triple the amount of the illegal profits in any case brought by the SEC. The law also provides for a bounty for informers in insider trading cases (10 percent of the illegal profits surrendered) and allows all investors who were trading in a stock while insiders were at work to sue for damages.

95

The new law clearly bolsters the enforcement powers of the SEC. However, the agency had hoped that Congress would provide a clear legal definition of insider trading. Insider trading is governed by the general antifraud provisions of the existing securities laws and is often difficult to prove in court. In the course of their work, everyone in the financial community hears rumors of impending deals and forms opinions as to which companies are ripe for takeover bids; so even though the timing of a profitable stock deal may look suspicious, it may have been based solely on shrewd analysis or an educated guess. The Wall Street professional will always have an advantage over the casual investor, because the professional is close to the action and devotes all of his or her working day to the markets. Unless someone confesses to passing privileged information or there is a clear pattern of trading, as in the Levine case, it is not always possible for prosecutors and juries to draw the line between cleverness and criminality.

Congressional leaders, on the other hand, were afraid that a narrow definition of insider trading would prove less effective than the current guidelines. In a field as complicated as securities law, ingenious people often find ways of cheating while satisfying all the technical requirements of the law. This makes it all the harder to get at them. Therefore, barring a change in congressional thinking, the SEC will have to make its own way in this murky area.

The SEC reacted quickly in November 1988 to the new insider trading legislation. The agency announced a change in its rules on the buying or selling of a company's stock by its own executives. Those defined as insiders are still barred from buying and then reselling their company's stock within a six-month period. But the new rule narrows the definition of who is an insider to include only a handful of top executives in each company. Thus, this apparent easing of the rules will, according to an analysis in the *New York Times*, enable the SEC "to concentrate its resources on prosecuting people who actually abuse insider information rather than monitoring all executives in a position to do so." This is a significant area of concern, because a company's top executives can be the ultimate insiders. They usually know well before the public when something happens that may affect the value of the company's stock, and the SEC wants to avoid future Texas Gulf Sulphur cases.

Of course, the insider rules do not prevent someone from selling information to others, having an accomplice buy stock, or trading through a foreign bank under an assumed name, as Dennis Levine did. In May 1985 the SEC took its first punitive action against an individual who passed insider information without making a personal profit. The violator, a Cleveland investment banker, had tipped off three friends about the impending buyout of a drugstore chain. He paid a fine of nearly $500,000, and his friends were heavily fined by the SEC and forced to forfeit their illegal profits.

For the foreseeable future, the SEC clearly hopes that the example of the Levine, Boesky, and Drexel Burnham cases will have a deterrent effect. Corporations, investment banks, and law firms involved in takeovers have been adopting more and more elaborate measures to safeguard information about impending deals. Like characters in a spy novel, they commonly use code names in documents and conversations. Sometimes even high-ranking executives in a company involved in a takeover are kept in the dark until a day or two before the deal is completed. Nevertheless, according to a *New York Times* article, as of late 1988 inside information was still available on Wall Street—people just had to dig a little harder to find it. The threat of jail sentences had not abolished the practice of insider trading because, as one anonymous stock trader told the *Times*, "it's very, very tempting."

Market Regulation

The SEC's foremost concern in the coming years—and the foremost concern of the securities industry—will be the stability of the markets. The markets have rebounded fairly well from the 1987 crash, and some argue that the crash was simply the kind of natural "adjustment" that occurs when stock prices get too high. Be that as it may, the markets cannot afford too many adjustments that cost investors $500 billion in lost stock value. As a stock trader quoted by Tim Metz of the *Wall Street Journal* put it, in the midst of Black Monday: "How can a stock market exist that behaves like this? Who would risk capital to invest in such a market?" The SEC has undoubtedly asked this question many times. Based on its study of the crash, the agency subsequently submitted proposals to Congress that called for significant changes in the securities laws.

In what is perhaps its most dramatic proposal, the SEC is asking Congress for authority to suspend trading on the stock exchanges for 24 hours in any future emergency. With the approval of the president of the United States, the suspension could be continued for a longer period. This would be a significant departure, because the power to suspend trading has always resided with the exchanges themselves. John J. Phelan, Jr., the chairman and chief executive officer of the NYSE, has stated that he was prepared to close the NYSE during the 1987 crash if the SEC asked him to do it. SEC chairman David Ruder conferred by telephone with Phelan during the crisis, but neither man revealed

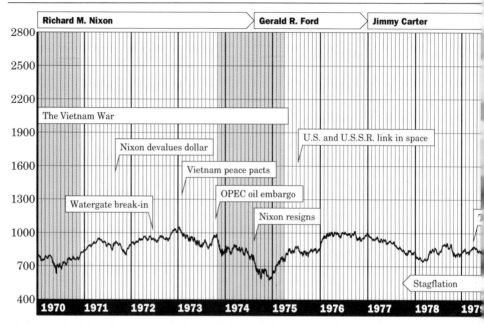

| | Richard M. Nixon | Gerald R. Ford | Jimmy Carter |

This graph of the Dow Jones Industrial Average juxtaposes historical events and stock market trends from 1970 to 1989. It also shows that the stock market recovered quickly after the crash in October 1987. The Dow, an index of 30 major stocks, is the most widely recognized indicator of the general level and trend of the stock market.

anything about the decisions that were made. Whatever passed between Phelan and Ruder, the SEC clearly feels that the present arrangement is not sufficient to protect the market in future crises.

A second proposal would require the NYSE to report immediately any stock trade that exceeds a certain limit—5 million shares would be a likely figure. Under the proposed regulation, the NYSE would also be obliged to reveal the name of the trader to the SEC, something it is not currently required to do. (Congress would make this information exempt from the Freedom of Information Act so that the SEC would not itself be required to make it public.)

The SEC wants to scrutinize large trades because they have a powerful effect on the market. One of the principal causes of the 1987 crash is thought to have been the automatic selling by computer of large blocks of stock. This practice is known as *program trading*, because the computers of investment firms are programmed to sell on certain accounts when prices drop below a specified level. Program trading is designed to prevent *institutional investors,*

98

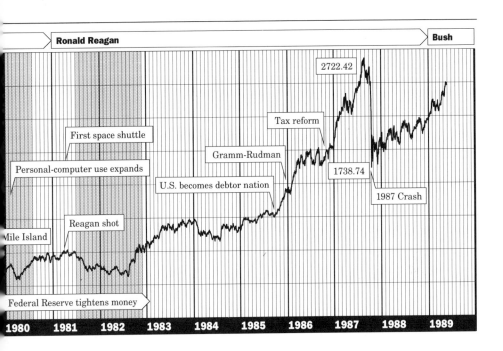

2722.42

Tax reform

First space shuttle

Gramm-Rudman

Personal-computer use expands

1738.74

U.S. becomes debtor nation

1987 Crash

Reagan shot

Mile Island

Federal Reserve tightens money

1980 1981 1982 1983 1984 1985 1986 1987 1988 1989

such as pension funds, insurance companies, and mutual funds, who may have hundreds of millions of dollars at stake, from losing too much when stock prices decline. This is a reasonable procedure in theory. But in practice, when many large investors begin to sell at the same time, the effect on the entire market can be disastrous. Other investors are afraid to buy when they see prices going down, and without any buyers the market can plunge into a free-fall, as it did on Black Monday. In any future scenario of this kind, the SEC would like to be in a position to take quick action without having to wait for notification by the NYSE.

The NYSE is not battling the SEC as it did during the 1930s. On the contrary, the NYSE has tightened its own rules in response to the events of 1987. It has prohibited program trading when stock prices go beyond a certain limit in either direction and has placed restrictions on brokers' ability to trade on their own accounts. The NYSE computers are programmed to "flag" large trades, and, like all exchanges, the NYSE reports anything suspicious to the SEC (although it still protects the identity of traders). But the SEC obviously feels that as long as the NYSE is a private organization, its first priority will always be the well-being of its members—and so the SEC continues to desire a greater presence on the exchange floor.

After the 1987 crash, John J. Phelan, Jr., chairman of the NYSE since 1984, oversaw adoption of exchange reforms such as limits on program trading.

The SEC's most controversial proposal is to have Congress extend SEC jurisdiction to trading in stock index futures and options. Trading in index futures and index options allows investors to hedge their bets on the performance of the market. Instead of taking a total risk by buying or selling a stock, the investor can take a partial risk by buying or selling a contract to deal in the stock at some future time. By waiting to see whether stock prices go up or down, the investor can then decide whether it is better to fulfill the contract or let the contract expire and lose only the initial fee paid to the other party. Some investors "straddle" the market by buying and selling different kinds of contracts at the same time. These are complicated maneuvers, and those who understand them can usually make money in any kind of market.

The SEC has never regulated trading in index futures and index options because this kind of trading does not involve the actual transfer of securities. It is considered to be *commodities trading*, the same as the trading that takes place in contracts to deliver specific quantities of cattle, corn, soybeans, hogs, gold, silver, currency, and other products. Commodities trading is centered in Chicago and is regulated by the Commodity Futures Trading Commission (CFTC), a federal agency created in 1974. Restrictions imposed by the CFTC are less severe than those imposed on the securities markets, and the CFTC has at times been dismissed, in the words of *Business Week*, as a "puppy-dog regulator."

In its report on the 1987 crash, the SEC concluded that futures trading in Chicago had a powerful effect on the NYSE. As soon as stock prices began to slip, investors started trading contracts in Chicago in a way that showed they expected prices to keep on falling. When news of this reached New York, it produced what the SEC termed a "negative market psychology." The SEC firmly believes that the futures market and the securities market are really one big market and that it cannot regulate one segment without regulating the other. The CFTC naturally does not share this opinion. But the Federal Bureau of Investigation's announcement in 1989 that it had uncovered widespread criminal activity on the Chicago commodities markets is likely to bolster the SEC's case.

As the securities markets develop through the 1990s and into the 21st century, many changes will surely take place. For more than 20 years, some economists and regulators have called for the creation of a single national securities market. Under this plan, the different exchanges would simply cease to exist as physical entities. All trades would be done by computers, as they

Two Chicago brokers try to keep up with orders for stock index futures. The SEC has asked Congress to grant it authority to regulate trading in stock index futures, which the SEC believes has a powerful effect on the securities markets.

101

are done now in the OTC market. So far, no one has come up with a detailed and workable plan for such a national market. And most likely, the existing exchanges would battle this idea for all they are worth. If a central market is ever created, it is sure to eliminate some present concerns of the SEC and develop many new areas of regulation.

One thing that might be safely predicted is a continuing national debate about the proper way to regulate the securities markets. In the wake of the 1987 crash and the insider trading scandals, there will be many who prefer to see the SEC clamp down on Wall Street as hard as possible. Others would argue that because the securities markets have gone global, with round-the-clock trading on the Tokyo and London exchanges, U.S. companies need more leeway in order to keep up with foreign competitors. They would also insist that the U.S. economy, beset by unfavorable trade balances, needs a steady flow of capital in order to improve its performance. The SEC showed that it was sensitive to

Over-the-counter (OTC) brokers use the National Association of Securities Dealers Automatic Quotation System (NASDAQ) to execute trade orders of 500 or fewer shares. The NASD, which supervises all trading in the OTC market, operates under the guidance of the SEC.

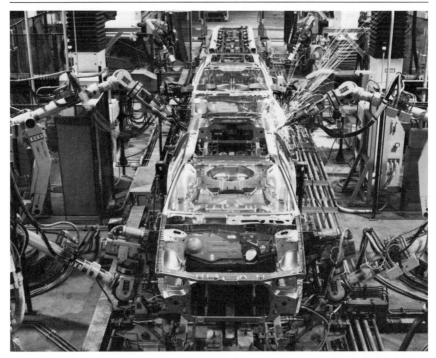

Taurus and Sable cars being assembled at Ford Motor Company's Chicago plant in 1987. The SEC endeavors to regulate the securities markets not only to prevent abuses but also to stimulate the flow of capital. If investors have confidence in the securities market, they will invest in businesses, which, in turn, will generate economic growth and prosperity.

these concerns by proposing in 1989 to relax its rules to allow an increase in private offerings of corporate bonds and foreign stocks to large investors. Such offerings are exempt from the usual disclosure rules and other time-consuming approval procedures. The SEC's action was expected to bring billions of dollars into the U.S. securities markets and was generally welcomed on Wall Street.

Whatever measures it adopts, the SEC will have a very hard time enforcing absolute honesty when there are such enormous amounts of money tempting people to break the rules. Regardless of its accomplishments, the agency will never be able to ensure that investors never make foolish decisions and never lose money playing the market. But if the SEC can continue to see that the average investor has a fair chance and that the markets provide a steady flow of capital into the economy, it will likely maintain its reputation as the most effective regulatory agency in the United States.

Securities and Exchange Commission

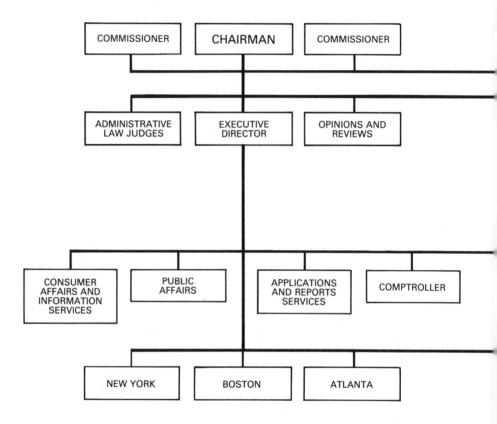

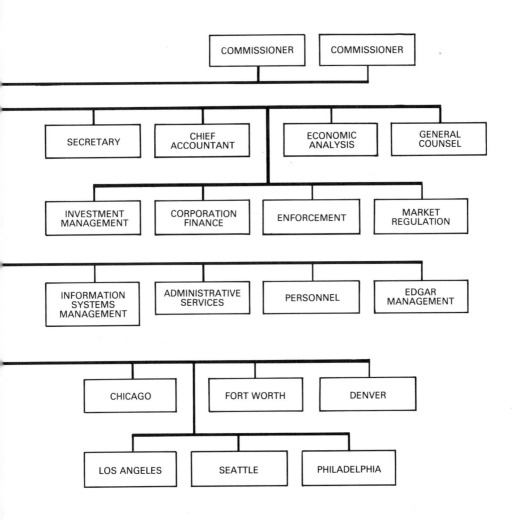

GLOSSARY

Annual report A report published by a corporation to inform investors of its performance during the preceding fiscal year.

ASRs (Accounting Series Releases) A series of documents issued by the Securities and Exchange Commission that keeps accountants up-to-date on the proper methods of reporting corporate financial information.

Bear market A phase of market activity during which stock prices consistently fall.

Blue-sky laws State laws that protect investors by prohibiting the misrepresentation of securities. These laws require that specific information be given to prospective investors.

Bond A certificate that represents a loan to a company. The issuing company (the borrower) pays interest for the use of the money and must repay the entire amount of the bond at a specified time.

Bull market A phase of market activity during which stock prices consistently rise.

Churning A stockbroker's illegal practice of buying and selling clients' securities for the primary purpose of generating commissions.

Commission brokers Agents who act as intermediaries between buyers and sellers of securities and who charge a commission, or percentage of the total price, on each transaction.

Commodities trading The buying and selling of contracts for goods—such as agricultural products, livestock, and metals—to be delivered at a specified future time and at a specified price.

EDGAR (Electronic Data Gathering Analysis and Retrieval) A computer system that the SEC is developing to make information more readily available to the public and the financial community.

Floor traders Speculators who have purchased a seat on an exchange and who buy and sell stocks strictly for themselves.

Holding company   A company that is created for the sole purpose of controlling and trading the stocks of other companies.

Insider trading   Stock transactions that are illegal because they take advantage of important information not available to the public.

Margin account   An account in which an investor deposits a minimum amount of money for the purchase of securities, borrowing the remainder from a broker. In exchange for margin credit, the investor pays interest to the broker.

Mutual fund   An investment in which the money of many shareholders is combined in order to invest in a wide range of securities.

NASDAQ   (pronounced "naz·dak") The computerized National Association of Securities Dealers Automatic Quotations system, which provides price quotations on stocks and bonds traded over the counter. The National Association of Securities Dealers (NASD) is the organization of brokers who handle the securities traded over the counter.

OTC market (over-the-counter market)   The nationwide network of brokers who handle transactions of stock that are not listed on an exchange.

Registration statement   A document containing financial disclosure information that issuers of securities are required to send to the SEC before the sale of a new security.

Securities   Stock certificates or bonds that are evidence of property or debt.

Share of stock   Any of the equal parts into which the entire value of a company is divided. It represents part ownership in the company.

Stock exchange   A market in which securities are sold at prices determined by supply and demand. The New York Stock Exchange, American Stock Exchange, and the over-the-counter market are the major U.S. exchanges.

Stop order   An order issued by the SEC suspending the proposed issuance of securities when the agency has determined that the disclosure information contained in the registration statement is inadequate.

SELECTED REFERENCES

Brooks, John. *The Go-Go Years.* New York: Weybright and Talley, 1973.

———. *Once in Golconda: A True Drama of Wall Street, 1920–1938.* New York: Harper & Row, 1969.

Douglas, William O. *Go East, Young Man.* New York: Random House, 1974.

Frantz, Douglas. *Levine & Co.: Wall Street's Insider Trading Scandal.* New York: Henry Holt, 1987.

Louchheim, Katie, ed. *The Making of the New Deal: The Insiders Speak.* Cambridge: Harvard University Press, 1983.

McCraw, Thomas. *Prophets of Regulation.* Cambridge: Harvard University Press, 1984.

Metz, Tim. *Black Monday: The Catastrophe of October 19, 1987 . . . and Beyond.* New York: Morrow, 1988.

Parrish, Michael. *Securities Regulation and the New Deal.* New Haven: Yale University Press, 1970.

Ritchie, Donald A. *James M. Landis: Dean of the Regulators.* Cambridge: Harvard University Press, 1980.

Schwartz, Bernard. *The Economic Regulation of Business and Industry: A Legislative History of U.S. Regulatory Agencies.* New York: Chelsea House, 1973.

Seligman, Joel. *The Transformation of Wall Street.* Boston: Houghton Mifflin, 1982.

Shapiro, Susan. *Wayward Capitalists: Target of the Securities and Exchange Commission.* New Haven: Yale University Press, 1984.

Sobel, Robert. *The Big Board: A History of the New York Stock Market.* New York: Free Press, 1965.

———. *Inside Wall Street: Continuity and Change in the Financial District.* New York: Norton, 1982.

U.S. Securities and Exchange Commission. *The October 1987 Market Break.* Washington, DC: U.S. Government Printing Office, 1988.

INDEX

Philip Koslow holds B.A. and M.A. degrees in political science from New York University. He was an instructor in international affairs at Oxford University and has taught creative writing in the New York City public schools. He has also worked as a caseworker at the Department of Welfare in New York and as a free-lance writer and editor. He is currently an editor at a publishing house in New York City.

Arthur M. Schlesinger, jr., served in the White House as special assistant to Presidents Kennedy and Johnson. He is the author of numerous acclaimed works in American history and has twice been awarded the Pulitzer Prize. He taught history at Harvard College for many years and is currently Albert Schweitzer Professor of the Humanities at the City College of New York.